SCHOLASTIC

National Curriculum
MATHS
Revision Guide

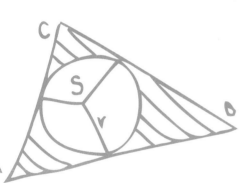

✓ Recap
✓ Revise
✓ Skills Check

Ages 10–11
Year 6

KS2

National Curriculum
MATHS
Revision Guide

Book End, Range Road, Witney, Oxfordshire, OX29 0YD
Registered office: Westfield Road, Southam, Warwickshire CV47 0RA
www.scholastic.co.uk

© 2016, Scholastic Ltd

6789 89012345

British Library Cataloguing-in-Publication Data
A catalogue record for this book is available from the British Library.

ISBN 978-1407-15990-4
Printed in Malaysia

Due to the nature of the web we cannot guarantee the content or links of any site mentioned. We strongly recommend that teachers check websites before using them in the classroom.

Author
Paul Hollin

Editorial
Rachel Morgan, Jenny Wilcox, Mark Walker, Red Door Media Ltd, Kate Baxter, Christine Vaughan and Julia Roberts

Series Design
Scholastic Design Team: Nicolle Thomas and Neil Salt

Design
Oxford Designers & Illustrators

Cover Design
Scholastic Design Team: Nicolle Thomas and Neil Salt

Cover Illustration
Shutterstock / © VIGE.CO

Illustration
Simon Walmesley

Contents

How to use this book

Introduction

This book has been written to help children reinforce the mathematics they have learned at school. It provides information and varied examples, activities and questions in a clear and consistent format across 42 units, covering all of National Curriculum for Mathematics for this age group.

I give tips to children and adults alike!

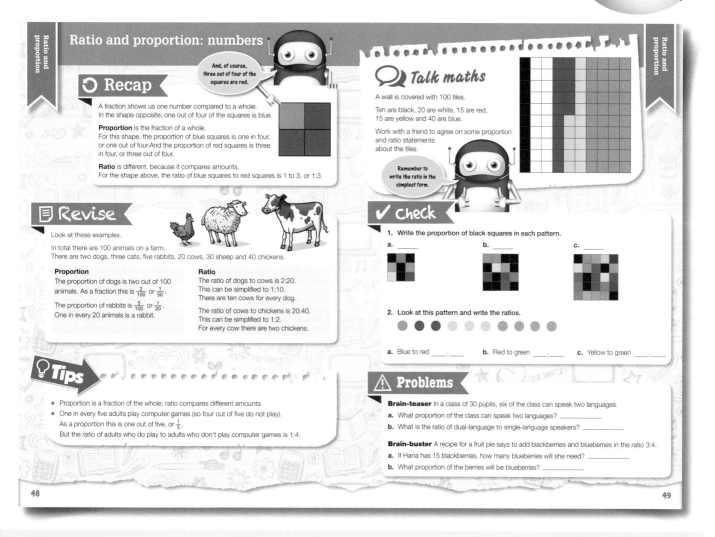

Unit structure

- **Recap** – a recap of basic facts of the mathematical area in focus.
- **Revise** – examples and facts specific to the age group.
- **Tips** – short and simple advice to aid understanding.
- **Talk maths** – focused activities that encourage verbal practice.
- **Check** – a focused range of questions, with answers at the end of the book.
- **Problems** – word problems requiring mathematics to be used in context.

Keep some blank or squared paper handy for notes and calculations!

Using this book at home

Improving your child's maths

It sounds obvious, but this is the best reason for using this book. Whether working sequentially through units, dipping in to resolve confusion, or reinforcing classroom learning, you can use this book to help your child see the benefits and pleasures of being competent in maths.

Consolidating school work

Most schools communicate clearly what they are doing each week via newsletters or homework. Using this book, alongside the maths being done at school, can boost children's mastery of the concepts. Be sure not to get ahead of schoolwork or to confuse your child. If in doubt, talk to your child's class teacher.

Revising for tests

Regular testing is a fact of life for children these days, like it or not. Improving children's confidence is a good way to avoid stress as well as improve performance. Where children have obvious difficulties, dipping in to the book and focusing on specific facts and skills can be very helpful.
To provide specific practice for end-of-year tests we recommend Scholastic Mathematics Practice Tests for Year 6.

Do a little, often

Keep sessions to an absolute maximum of 30 minutes. Even if children want to keep going, short amounts of focused study on a regular basis will help to sustain learning and enthusiasm in the long run.

Track progress

The revision tracker chart on page 7 provides a simple way for children to record their progress with this book. Remember, you've really 'got it' when you can understand and apply the maths confidently in different contexts. This means all the questions in the *Check* and *Problems* sections should not present any difficulties.

Avoid confusion

If your child really doesn't seem to understand a particular unit, take a step back. There may be some prior knowledge that s/he does not understand, or it may contradict how they have learned similar facts at school. Try looking at much simpler examples than those given in the book, and if in doubt talk to your child's teacher.

Talk, talk, talk

There is big value in discussing maths, both using vocabulary and explaining concepts. The more children can be encouraged to do this, especially explaining their thinking and understanding, the better the learning. Even if adults understand the work better than children, having them 'teach' you is a great way to consolidate their learning.

Practice makes perfect

Even the world's best footballers have to regularly practise kicking a ball. Brief warm ups before starting a unit, such as rapid recall of times tables or addition facts, or answering a few questions on mathematical vocabulary (see glossary) can help keep children on their toes.

Maths is everywhere – use it!

Children have lots of English lessons at school, and they use language almost constantly in daily life. They also have lots of maths lessons but encounter its use in daily life much less. Involving children in everyday maths is very useful. Shopping and money are the obvious ones, but cooking, decorating, planning holidays, catching buses, to name a few examples, can all involve important mathematical thinking and talk.

Revision tracker

	Not sure	Getting there	Got it!
Identify place value in numbers up to 1,000,000			
Work with numbers up to 10,000,000			
Round any whole to the nearest power of 10			
Use positive and negative numbers in practical contexts			
Use mental and written methods to add and subtract large numbers			
Use skills and knowledge to multiply and divide numbers mentally			
Perform long multiplication using formal written methods			
Perform short division using formal written methods			
Perform long division using formal written methods			
Perform operations in the correct order in complex calculations			
Identify and use factors, multiples and prime numbers			
Use common factors to simplify fractions			
Compare and order fractions with different denominators			
Add and subtract fractions			
Multiply proper fractions			
Divide proper fractions			
Convert between fractions and decimals			
Use decimals with up to three decimal places			
Multiply decimals by whole numbers			
Divide decimals by whole numbers			
Convert between fractions, decimals and percentages			
Use ratio and proportion to compare quantities			
Use percentages for comparison and problem solving			
Use scale factors to compare shapes			
Use simple formulae			
Use algebra to solve missing number problems			
Solve equations with two variables			
Solve problems for different measures using appropriate units			
Convert different units of measurement			
Calculate the perimeter and area of regular and composite shapes			
Use formulae to calculate areas			
Use formulae to calculate volumes			
Measure, construct and use different angles			
Identify 2D shapes from their properties			
Construct 2D shapes			
Identify 3D shapes and their nets			
Identify and draw the parts of a circle			
Work with coordinates in all four quadrants			
Reflect and translate shapes with positive and negative coordinates			
Construct and use pie charts			
Construct and use line graphs			
Calculate the mean of a data set			

The number system

The Romans didn't have zero or place value.

↻ Recap

In the past, some people used the Roman system when writing numbers. The Romans used letters to represent amounts.

Nowadays we use ten digits:

0 1 2 3 4 5 6 7 8 9

All of the maths we do only uses these ten digits.
We can do a lot with only ten digits because of **place value**.

📋 Revise

Our number system is called **base 10** because it arranges digits in columns that increase in powers of 10.

1,000,000s	100,000s	10,000s	1000s	100s	10s	1s
5	6	4	0	3	4	2

Notice how each digit represents a different amount depending on its place value.

💡 Tips

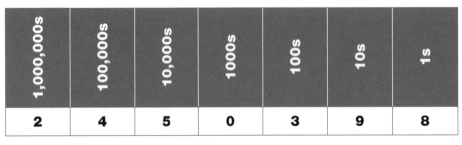

- Make sure you can read large numbers. It isn't so hard if you take your time. Look at this number:

  2450398

- We can separate the millions and thousands using gaps or commas.

  2,450,398 or **2 450 398**

There's certainly a place for gaps or commas!

- If you are still unsure, write in the place value above each digit.

1,000,000s	100,000s	10,000s	1000s	100s	10s	1s
2	4	5	0	3	9	8

Say it out aloud: two million, four hundred and fifty thousand, three hundred and ninety-eight.

💬 Talk maths

Roman numerals

Work with a partner. Challenge each other to say any Roman numeral up to 1000. The table below gives you everything you need to know.

Number	1	2	3	4	5	6	7	8	9	10
Roman numeral	I	II	III	IV	V	VI	VII	VIII	IX	X
Number	50	100	500	1000						
Roman numeral	L	C	D	M						

It's quite easy once you get the hang of it!

Base 10 numbers

Starting small and getting bigger, write down ten numbers up to 10,000,000 and challenge your partner to say them correctly.

349   9235   400,004   45,202
305,621   3,452,320   90,009
726,817   3,000,003   6,426,208

✔ Check

1. Change these Roman numerals to base 10 numbers.

   a. CCCL _____   b. CXC _____   c. MMMD _____   d. MDCLXVI _____

2. Write the value of the underlined digit in each number.

   a. 32,4<u>0</u>2 _____   b. 2<u>3</u>0,508 _____

   c. <u>4</u>,730,627 _____   d. 7,6<u>7</u>3,205 _____

⚠ Problems

Brain-teaser Write the number that is one more than one million. _____

Brain-buster What is the biggest 7-digit number? Write it in digits then in words.

_____

_____

Numbers to 10,000,000

↺ Recap

239,718 in words is two hundred and thirty-nine thousand, seven hundred and eighteen.

100,000s	10,000s	1000s	100s	10s	1s
2	3	9	7	1	8

The **place value** of the three digit represents 30,000; the seven represents 700. What do the other digits represent?

Zeros are also important.
402,005 in words is four hundred and two thousand and five.

100,000s	10,000s	1000s	100s	10s	1s
4	0	2	0	0	5

 Revise

This number is twelve million, seven hundred and sixty-four thousand, three hundred and five.

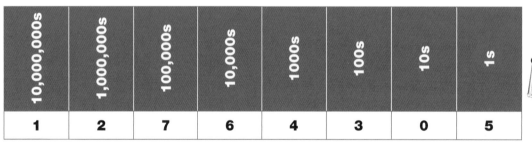

10,000,000s	1,000,000s	100,000s	10,000s	1000s	100s	10s	1s
1	2	7	6	4	3	0	5

Use commas after the millions and after the thousands column.
The number above should be written as 12,764, 305.

What number does each of the digits represent?

♀ Tips

- Write the place value in columns above numbers if you're stuck.
- < means less than and > means more than.

DID YOU KNOW?

A billion is a thousand million. One billion has nine zeros.

Talk maths

With a partner, practise saying these numbers.

10,000	10,000,000	5,999,999 < 6,000,001
100,000	7,291,428	2,450,312 > 1,974,489
1,000,000	21,426,3007	9,999,999

DID YOU KNOW?

1000² (one thousand squared) = 1,000,000

✔ Check

1. **Write this number in words.** 845,283

_____

2. **Write this number using digits.**

six hundred and four thousand, one hundred and ninety _____

3. **What does the 6 digit represent in 3,682,309?** _____

4. **Put these numbers in order, from smallest to largest.**

825,421   10,000,000   97,612   6,899,372   500,000

_____ _____ _____ _____ _____

5. **Insert the < or > sign between each pair to make the number statements correct.**

a. 3521 _____ 5630   **b.** 15,204 _____ 9798   **c.** 833,521 _____ 795,732

⚠ Problems

City	Rome	Paris	Madrid
Population	2,646,346	2,341,895	3,324,031

Brain-teaser Which city has the largest population? _____

Brain-buster Write the names of these cities in order, from smallest population to largest population.

_____ _____ _____

Estimation and rounding

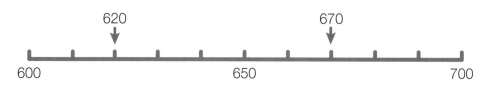

We use powers of 10 for rounding, counting and estimating.

↻ Recap

To round a number to the nearest **power of 10** we look at it on a number line.

620   670
↓   ↓
600   650   700

620 rounded down to the nearest hundred is 600   670 rounded up is 700

649 and below will round down to 600; 650 and above round up to 700.

We can count on in 100s too: 100, 200, 300, 400, 500 and so on.

And we can also use these skills to estimate answers, for example,
103 + 98 + 204 + 195 = is approximately 100 + 100 + 200 + 200 = 600

📑 Revise

We can do the same with thousands and millions.

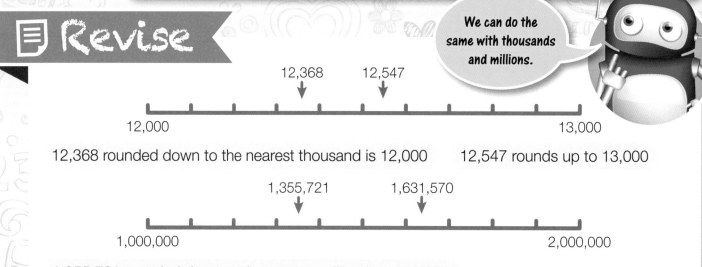

12,368   12,547
↓   ↓
12,000   13,000

12,368 rounded down to the nearest thousand is 12,000   12,547 rounds up to 13,000

1,355,721   1,631,570
↓   ↓
1,000,000   2,000,000

1,355,721 rounded down to the nearest million is 1,000,000

1,631,570 rounds up to 2,000,000

To estimate the answer to 45,231 + 23,876 we could say 45,000 + 24,000 = 69,000.
To estimate the answer to 7,235,421 − 5,862,403 we could say
7,000,000 − 6,000,000 = 1,000,000.

💡 Tips

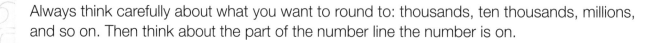

Always think carefully about what you want to round to: thousands, ten thousands, millions, and so on. Then think about the part of the number line the number is on.

Talk maths

Work with a partner. Each write six different numbers between 10,000 and 10,000,000. Say aloud each other's numbers and then challenge each other to round any of the numbers to a power of 10.

What is 5,348,325 rounded to the nearest 100,000?

✔ Check

1. Round these numbers to the nearest 1000.

   a. 4567 _____

   b. 23,145 _____

   c. 45,320 _____

   d. 78,649 _____

2. Round these numbers to the nearest 100,000.

   a. 120,367 _____

   b. 450,000 _____

   c. 1,382,320 _____

   d. 7,976,311 _____

3. Round these numbers to the nearest 1,000,000.

   a. 6,435,207 _____

   b. 845,453 _____

   c. 3,500,000 _____

   d. 9,724,500 _____

4. Complete these sequences.

   a. 0; 100,000; 200,000; _____; _____; _____;

   b. 370,000; 380,000; _____; _____; _____;

   c. 7,500,000; 8,500,000; _____; _____; _____;

⚠ Problems

Brain-teaser Round each city's population to the nearest million.

City	Rome	Paris	Madrid
Population	2,646,346	2,341,895	3,324,031

Rome _____   Paris _____   Madrid _____

Brain-buster Estimate, to the nearest million, the total population of Madrid, Rome and Paris.

_____

Do you think your estimate is higher or lower than the actual total? Explain your answer.

_____

_____

13

Negative numbers

↻ Recap

Numbers can be negative as well as positive.

–10 –9 –8 –7 –6 –5 –4 –3 –2 –1 0 1 2 3 4 5 6 7 8 9 10

Remember you can use a number line to help you. Don't forget to include zero when you are counting!

📄 Revise

Temperature is a great way to practise using positive and negative numbers.

If you start at +2 and count back 6 you stop at –4.

If you start at +15 and count back 16 you end at –1.

If you start at –8 and count on 16 you stop at +8.

If you start at –13 and count on 24 you stop at +11.

We can do simple calculations with positive and negative numbers to check the answer. For example:

$2 - 3 = -1$ **so** $-3 + 2 = -1$ $-14 + 18 = 4$ **so** $18 - 14 = 4$

You just need to remember to swap the minus to a positive and the positive to a negative.

```
+20
+18
+16
+14
+12
+10
+8
+6
+4
+2
0
-2
-4
-6
-8
-10
-12
-14
-16
-18
-20
```

💡 Tips

- Can you spot the connections between positive and negative numbers? Look at the connections in the box. If you understand this, negative numbers will be easy for you!

$8 - 4 = 4$	$4 + 8 = 12$	$12 - 8 = 4$	$12 - 8 = 4$
$4 - 8 = -4$	$-4 - 8 = -12$	$8 - 12 = -4$	$4 - 12 = -8$

- Try choosing some other numbers and see if you can spot patterns.

Talk maths

> What's minus ten plus fifteen?

> Minus five.

7	9	12
4	16	20
−3	−12	−8
−20	−17	−5

With a partner, choose two numbers from the box and ask them to either subtract or add them together. For example, say: *What is nine minus twelve?* Now ask them to ask you some questions. Use the number line below to help you.

−20 −19 −18 −17 −16 −15 −14 −13 −12 −11 −10 −9 −8 −7 −6 −5 −4 −3 −2 −1 0 1 2 3 4 5 6 7 8 9 10 11 12 13 14 15 16 17 18 19 20

✔ Check

1. Complete these calculations.

   a. $3 − 5 =$ _____   **b.** $5 − 9 =$ _____   **c.** $−4 + 7 =$ _____   **d.** $−8 + 8 =$ _____

2. Count on from −20 to +20 in steps of 4. Write each number.

   _____ _____ _____ _____ _____ _____ _____ _____ _____ _____ _____

3. Write the missing signs + or −.

   a. 7 _____ $7 = 0$ 　　　　　　　　**b.** $−12$ _____ $13 = 1$

   c. 14 _____ $21 = −7$ 　　　　　　**d.** 2 _____ $18 = −16$

4. Write the missing numbers.

   a. $−13 +$ _____ $= 1$ 　**b.** $14 −$ _____ $= −5$ 　**c.** _____ $− 15 = −8$ 　**d.** _____ $+ 10 = 1$

⚠ Problems

Brain-teaser One winter morning the temperature at dawn is −4 degrees Celsius (−4°C). If the temperature rises 12°C by noon, what will the temperature be then?

_____

Brain-buster The temperature in the desert 49.7°C and in the mountains is −19.7°C.

What is the difference between the two places? _____

DID YOU KNOW?

Even though deserts are hot places, they can get very cold at night.

15

Addition and subtraction

> To add 999, just add 1000 and subtract 1.
> 45,362 + 999 = 46,361.

↺ Recap

You will probably know several mental methods for addition and subtraction.

You must learn your number bonds: 7 + 8 = 15   15 − 8 = 7   15 − 7 = 8
Partitioning numbers is important too: 25 + 12 = 37

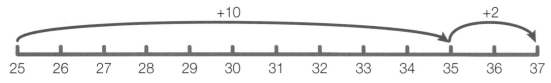

📄 Revise

We can use formal written methods for adding and subtracting larger numbers.

The first step is to neatly lay out the numbers in columns according to place value.

```
    6 6 4 5 7 2
  + 1 5 3 0 5 4
  -------------
    8 1 7 6 2 6
        ₁     ₁
```

Just like addition, we can use the place-value columns to subtract larger numbers.

```
  ²3̶ ¹³4̶ ¹⁰4̶ ¹2 4 6
  - 1 6 5 3 0 4
  -------------
    1 7 5 9 4 2
```

If in doubt, ask someone to show you.

💡 Tips

- Remember, you can check your subtractions by adding your answer to the number you took away.

```
  ¹2̶ ¹3 ³4̶ ¹³4̶ ¹3
  -   6 1 7 5
  -----------
    1 7 2 6 8    checking…

    1 7 2 6 8
  +   6 1 7 5
  -----------
    2 3 4 4 3    correct! ☺
    ₁   ₁ ₁
```

- Only use written methods that you are sure you understand. If you have a method you like, stick to it, practise it, and always check your answers!

Try it with three numbers, or even four!

💬 Talk maths

Think of two numbers and write them down. Challenge a friend to add them using a mental or written method, and then explain their method to you. Repeat this five or six times, then do the same for subtractions.

✔ Check

1. Add these numbers using mental methods.

   a. 452 + 340 = _____   **b.** 5127 + 399 = _____   **c.** 425,364 + 54,005 = _____

2. Subtract these numbers using mental methods.

   a. 800 − 260 = _____   **b.** 146,450 − 29,000 = _____   **c.** 2,754 − 399 = _____

3. Add these numbers using a written method.

   a. 234,482 + 314,222   **b.** 635,231 + 327,594   **c.** 1,342,435 + 3,825,032

4. Subtract these numbers using a written method.

   a. 314,222 − 234,482   **b.** 962,825 − 327,594   **c.** 3,825,032 − 1,342,435

⚠ Problems

City	Rome	Paris	Madrid
Population	2,646,346	2,341,895	3,324,031

Brain-teaser How many more people live in Madrid than Paris? _____

Brain-buster Calculate the combined population of Rome, Paris and Madrid. _____

Multiplication and division facts and skills

×	1	2	3	4	5	6	7	8	9	10	11	12
1	1	2	3	4	5	6	7	8	9	10	11	12
2	2	4	6	8	10	12	14	16	18	20	22	24
3	3	6	9	12	15	18	21	24	27	30	33	36
4	4	8	12	16	20	24	28	32	36	40	44	48
5	5	10	15	20	25	30	35	40	45	50	55	60
6	6	12	18	24	30	36	42	48	54	60	66	72
7	7	14	21	28	35	42	49	56	63	70	77	84
8	8	16	24	32	40	48	56	64	(72)	80	88	96
9	9	18	27	36	45	54	63	72	81	90	99	108
10	10	20	30	40	50	60	70	80	90	100	110	120
11	11	22	33	44	55	66	77	88	99	110	121	132
12	12	24	36	48	60	72	84	96	108	120	132	144

↺ Recap

Multiplication squares show us that division is the *inverse* of multiplication.

So, we can say:

$8 \times 9 = 72$

$9 \times 8 = 72$

$72 \div 9 = 8$

$72 \div 8 = 9$

Revise

You already know some square and cube number facts, and you can calculate others.

Five squared = $5^2 = 5 \times 5 = 25$

Five cubed = $5^3 = 5 \times 5 \times 5 = 125$

Remember the inverses: $25 \div 5 = 5$, $125 \div 5 = 25$

Also, you should now be able to multiply and divide by **powers of 10**.

Operation	Fact	Example
×10	Move one place left	$65 \times 10 = 650$
÷10	Move one place right	$65 \div 10 = 6.5$
×1000	Move three places left	$65 \times 1000 = 65,000$
÷1000	Move three places right	$65 \div 1000 = 0.065$
×1,000,000	Move six places left	$65 \times 1,000,000 = 65,000,000$
÷1,000,000	Move six places right	$65 \div 1,000,000 = 0.000065$

💡 Tips

When multiplying by larger numbers, we can separate the powers of 10, for example:

$7 \times 12,000$ is the same as $7 \times 12 \times 1000$
$= 84 \times 1000 = 84,000$

Or for $24,000 \div 6$, just do $24 \div 6 = 4$, then times by 1000
$= 4 \times 1000 = 4000$

🗨 Talk maths

Try to out-smart an adult. Ask them to solve a calculation mentally, then give them a challenge such as to multiply a square or cube number by a power of 10. For example:

What is seven squared times a thousand?

What is three cubed times one hundred thousand?

If you are feeling brave, work out some answers in advance and then try out-smarting an adult with a mental division, for example:

What is forty-nine thousand divided by seven?

What is two thousand seven hundred divided by three?

✔ Check

1. Solve these multiplications mentally.

   a. $24 \times 200 =$ _____

   b. $62 \times 1000 =$ _____

   c. $40 \times 40 =$ _____

   d. $25 \times 2000 =$ _____

   e. $43 \times 10,000 =$ _____

   f. $100 \times 10,000 =$ _____

2. Now solve these divisions using mental methods.

   a. $6000 \div 3 =$ _____

   b. $125 \div 5 =$ _____

   c. $120,000 \div 3 =$ _____

   d. $360,000 \div 4 =$ _____

   e. $640,008 \div 8 =$ _____

   f. $125,000 \div 5 =$ _____

3. Use your knowledge of inverses to solve these.

   a. If $27,072 \div 576 = 47$, what does $576 \times 47 =$ _____

   b. If $4320 \times 723 = 3,123,360$, what does $3,123,360 \div 4320 =$ _____

⚠ Problems

Brain-teaser A football stadium holds 8000 people. How much money would be collected for a sell-out match if each ticket was £20?

_____

Brain-buster For a different football match, tickets are sold for £30, but only £90,000 is collected.

How many tickets were sold? _____

Written methods for long multiplication

Remember, the numbers are arranged in their place-value columns: hundreds, tens and ones.

↻ Recap

There are several formal written methods for multiplying numbers. You may have been taught methods a bit different from this one. You should use whichever method you are comfortable with.

	3	6	
×	2	4	
1	4²	4		(← × 4)
7¹	2	0	+	(← × 20)
8	6	4	

Answer: 864

	4	7	
×	1	8	
3	7⁵	6		(← × 8)
4	7	0	+	(← × 10)
8	4	6	

Answer: 846

▤ Revise

We can use formal written methods for all numbers, no matter how large they are.
Multiplying two numbers that are both larger than 10 is called long multiplication.
We multiply each digit on the top by each digit on the bottom, carrying forward powers of 10.

		3	2	6	
	×		4	5	
	1	6¹	3³	0		(← × 5)
1	3¹	0²	4	0	+	(← × 40)
1	4	6	7	0	

Answer: 14,670

		4	2	0	8	
	×			6	3	
	1	2	6	2²	4		(← × 3)
2	5¹	2	4⁴	8	0	+	(← × 60)
2	6	5	1	0	4	

Answer: 265,104

Remember, always put the larger number on the top.

💡 Tips

Lay out your work neatly and you'll probably get the right answer.

Watch how to do huge calculations and get them right!

		8	6	9	5	
	×			6	7	
	6	0⁴	8⁶	6³	5		(← × 7)
5	2⁴	1⁵	7³	0	0	+	(← × 60)
5	8	2	5	6	5	

Answer: 582,565

💬 Talk maths

Look at each of these long multiplications and talk it through aloud, explaining how each stage was done. Make sure you work in the correct order.

		4	8	
	×	3	1	
		4	8	
1	4^2	4	0	+
1	4	8	8	

Answer: 1488

			6	0	7	
		×		2	5	
		3	0	3^3	5	
1	2	1^1	4	0		+
1	5	1	7	5		

Answer: 15,175

> Remember that zeros still have to be multiplied and recorded, and anything times zero is... zero!

✔ Check

1. Complete each of these long multiplications using a written method.

a. 62 × 14

b. 325 × 22

c. 405 × 34

d. 6338 × 52

2. Complete each of these long multiplications using a written method.

a. 425 × 21

b. 1267 × 30

c. 5326 × 15

d. 8736 × 65

⚠ Problems

Brain-teaser A head teacher estimates that every child in her school does 72 pieces of homework each year (that is around two pieces per week). If there are 347 children in the school, how many pieces of homework must be marked each year?

_____

Brain-buster A supermarket chain sells 9237 RoboDog toys in a year. They cost £79 each.

How much money does the supermarket make in total? _____

Written methods for short division

↺ Recap

There are several formal written methods for dividing numbers. You may have been taught methods a bit different to those in this book. You should use whichever method you are comfortable with – as long as you get the right answers!

		0	8	6
	3	2	²5	¹8

Answer: 258 ÷ 3 = 86

For 72 ÷ 8 = 9 we say, 72 **divided by** 8 equals 9.

📋 Revise

In short division we carry forward remainders. Sometimes there is a remainder in the answer at the end.

		0	6	3	r1
	4	2	²5	¹3	

Answer: 253 ÷ 4 = 63 r1

		0	2	2	5	r2
	7	1	¹5	¹7	³7	

Answer: 1577 ÷ 7 = 225 r2

💡 Tips

- Lay out your work carefully and think about the place value of every digit. Use squared paper to help you.

		0	8	5	8	6	9	r1
	3	2	²5	¹7	²6	²0	²8	

Answer: 257,608 ÷ 3 = 85,869 r1

- You can check your answer by multiplying the answer by the number you divided by, and then add the remainder. Look:

	8	5	8	6	9
×					3
2	5	7	6	0	7
		1	2	2	2

Answer: 257,607 + 1 remainder = 257,608

💬 Talk maths

Look at this short division and explain it aloud, saying how each stage was done.

	1	4	5	2	0	0	5	r4
6	8	²7	³1	¹2	0	3	³4	

Answer: 8,712,034 ÷ 6 = 1,452,005 r4

✔ Check

1. Complete each of these short divisions.

a. 92 ÷ 4

b. 123 ÷ 5

c. 2605 ÷ 6

d. 3758 ÷ 12

2. Complete each of these short divisions using a written method.

a. 86 ÷ 7

b. 322 ÷ 5

c. 3685 ÷ 8

d. 13,588 ÷ 12

⚠ Problems

Brain-teaser A teacher shares out 93 stickers between seven children. How many stickers will each child receive, and how many will be left over? _____

Brain-buster Tickets for a pop concert cost £18 each. If the total amount taken for tickets was £22,464,

how many tickets were sold? _____

Explain how you could check your answer.

_____

_____

THE NATIONAL ARENA ∧∧

THE SQUIDS

SAT, 8TH SEPT 2015
STALLS, PRICE: £18.00

£18.00

∧∧

Written methods for long division

Turn back a page to see formal methods for short division.

↺ Recap

To divide something means to share it into equal amounts. Twelve divided by three equals four.

For larger numbers we sometimes need to use formal methods to help us calculate accurate answers.

In short division we carry on the remainder at each stage.

		0	4	2	6	r2
8	3	³4	²1	⁵0		

Answer: 426 r2

📄 Revise

When we are dividing larger numbers we may need to use long division. This example shows you one method.

Can you see the difference between long division and short division? With long division we are calculating the remainder at each stage, so that there is less chance of making an error.

Whichever method you use, make sure you understand it!

					2	2	3	r3
		1	6	3	5	7	1	
(2 × 16 =)	−			3	2			
					3	7		
(2 × 16 =)	−				3	2		
						5	1	
(3 × 16 =)	−					4	8	
							3	

Answer: 223 r3

💡 Tips

Here's a bit of friendly advice about remainders.

- In calculations it is fine to leave a remainder, but in problem solving these need to be presented carefully. You may need to show the remainder, write the remainder as a fraction or a decimal, or round off the answer.

  For example: If five pizzas are shared between four people, you wouldn't say each person receives one pizza remainder one. You would say they get $1\frac{1}{4}$ pizzas each.

Or, if a problem asks how many rows of ten can 93 seats be arranged in, the answer is nine. We round the answer and ignore the remainder.

💬 Talk maths

Look at this long division and explain it aloud, saying how each stage was done.

Now try writing down and explaining the steps for this long division:
2878 ÷ 13

> **Remember** that zero divided by anything is ...zero.

			2	2	1	r5
	1	3	2	8	7	8
(2 × 13 =)	–		2	6		
				2	7	
(2 × 13 =)	–			2	6	
					1	8
(1 × 13 =)	–				1	3
						5

Answer: 221 r5

✔ Check

1. Complete each of these long divisions.

   a.

2	5	5	2	6	4	

   b.

1	5	3	8	1	8	

2. On squared paper, complete each of these long divisions using a written method.

   a. 338 ÷ 15   b. 4438 ÷ 21   c. 6358 ÷ 18   d. 7318 ÷ 32

⚠ Problems

Brain-teaser A theatre has 2010 seats.
If there are 15 seats per row, how many rows are there? _____

Brain-buster Sixteen people buy a lottery ticket and, altogether, they win £37,468. They agree to share it equally. How much will they each receive, to the nearest 1p? _____

Ordering operations

↺ Recap

Calculations and problems involving more than one operation are called **multi-step**.

You must only do one calculation at a time, and you must do them in the right order!

The right order is division and multiplication first, followed by addition and subtraction, working from left to right.

Look at this calculation:
$$25 \div 5 + 3 \times 7 - 6 \times 4$$

Division first $(25 \div 5 = 5)$	$5 + 3 \times 7 - 6 \times 4$
Multiplication next $(3 \times 7 = 21)$	$5 + 21 - 6 \times 4$
And another multiplication $(6 \times 4 = 24)$	$5 + 21 - 24$
Then addition $(5 + 21 = 26)$	$26 - 24$
And last subtraction $(26 - 24 = 2)$	Answer $= 2$

📋 Revise

Brackets make a big difference.

You can control the order in which calculations are done by using brackets. Calculations inside brackets come first. Look at this example:

$18 - 3 \times 5 = 18 - 15 = 3$ But $(18 - 3) \times 5 = 15 \times 5 = 75$

Or this one:

$21 \div 3 + 4 = 7 + 4 = 11$ But $21 \div (3 + 4) = 21 \div 7 = 3$

💡 Tips

Here's a top tip to keep your maths in order.

- If you understand this you are ready for **BIDMAS**:
  Brackets
  Indices (such as square and cube numbers)
  Division ⎤ Do multiplication and division together in the
  Multiplication ⎦ ← order they come, left to right.
  Addition ⎤ Do addition and subtraction together in the
  Subtraction ⎦ ← order they come, left to right.
- Indices are a bit tricky. They tell us the power of a number, for example, a square number such as 7^2 is 7 to the power of 2; 7^3 is 7 to the power of 3 and so on.

💬 Talk maths

Look at the calculation below. Try inserting a pair of brackets in different places and discuss, with a partner, what answer it gives you. Remember, do only one calculation at a time, and think BIDMAS.

$$24 + 48 \div 8 - 2 \times 5 - 4 =$$

✔ Check

1. Solve these.

   a. $24 \div 2 - 3 \times 4 =$ _____
   b. $23 - 7 \times 2 - 18 \div 6 =$ _____
   c. $3 \times 45 \div 5 =$ _____

2. Now solve these.

   a. $16 \div (3 + 5) =$ _____
   b. $47 - 7 \times (18 \div 6 + 2) =$ _____
   c. $(7 + 8) \div (12 - 9) =$ _____

3. Mark each of these calculations right (✓) or wrong (✗).

   a. $5 \times 3 - 14 \div 2 = 8$ _____
   b. $(25 - 6) \times 10 \div 5 = 38$ _____
   c. $(8 + 6) - 15 \div 5 \times (4 + 3) = 77$ _____
   d. $(3 \times 7 - 45 \div 5) + 22 - 88 \div (5 + 2 \times 3) = 26$ _____

4. Add the missing brackets to complete calculation correctly.

   a. $8 \times 5 + 2 - 3 = 53$
   b. $14 \div 7 + 2 \times 11 - 6 = 12$
   c. $64 - 12 + 5 \times 3 = 37$

⚠ Problems

Brain-teaser The prize for a charity raffle is £20. Tickets cost £2 each. Charlie sells 34 tickets, Georgina sells 17 tickets and Jayden sells 43 tickets. Georgina says they have made a profit of £168.

Is she right? _____

Write the calculation needed to work out the profit. _____

Brain-buster A car showroom sells new cars for £12,000. It also buys second-hand cars for £2,500 and sells them for £7,000. At the end of a week, the car showroom has received £37,500. Explain how many new cars have been sold, and how many second-hand cars have been bought and sold.

Write the calculation then work out the answer. _____

Factors, multiples and prime numbers

↺ Recap

A **multiple** is a number that is made by multiplying two numbers.

$$5 \times 7 = 35$$

35 is a multiple of both **5** and **7**.
We can also say that 5 and 7 are factors of 35.

Factors are easy to list in pairs:
The factors of 35 are 1 and 35, 5 and 7.
Factors are the numbers that we multiply together to get multiples.

Prime numbers can only be divided by themselves and one.

DID YOU KNOW?

A *titanic* prime is a prime number that has over 1000 digits!

Remember, 1 is not a prime number, and 2 is the only even prime number.

📋 Revise

A **common factor** is a factor shared by two or more numbers. For example 7 is a common factor of 14 and 77.

A **common multiple** is a multiple shared by two or more numbers. For example 20 is a common multiple of 2 and 5 (and of 1, 4, 10 and 20).

Factors and multiples are easy if you really know your times tables. Try to learn your primes up to 100.

Prime numbers on a 100-square

1	②	③	4	⑤	6	⑦	8	9	10
⑪	12	⑬	14	15	16	⑰	18	⑲	20
21	22	㉓	24	25	26	27	28	㉙	30
㉛	32	33	34	35	36	㊲	38	39	40
㊶	42	㊸	44	45	46	㊼	48	49	50
51	52	㊷	54	55	56	57	58	㊾	60
㊿	62	63	64	65	66	㊻	68	69	70
㉛	72	㉓	74	75	76	77	78	㊴	80
81	82	㊓	84	85	86	87	88	㊙	90
91	92	93	94	95	96	㊐	98	99	100

💡 Tips

- Remember that factors always come in pairs. It can help to list them in pairs too, for example:

  Look at 96 (it has the most factors for any number under 100, 12 altogether):

  96 = 1 × 96, 2 × 48, 3 × 32, 4 × 24, 6 × 16, 8 × 12

Talk maths

Play *True or False* with a partner. Spend ten minutes writing down a collection of facts about factors, multiples and primes, and then take turns challenging your partner to decide if your facts are true or false.

If you give false facts you must know what the true answer should be.

24 has eight factors (True: 1, 2, 3, 4, 6, 8, 12, 24)

100 is a common multiple of 4, 5 and 6 (False: 100 is not a multiple of 6)

38 has two prime factors (True: 2 and 19 are both prime numbers)

✔ Check

1. What are the common factors of 12 and 20? _____

2. What are the common factors of 30 and 50? _____

3. Write three common multiples of 3 and 5. _____

4. What is the lowest common multiple of 2, 5 and 7? _____

5. 30 has three prime factors. What are they? _____

6. What is the largest number between 1 and 100 that has two prime factors? _____

⚠ Problems

Brain-teaser David says, "2 is a prime number and 19 is a prime number. 2 × 19 = 38, so 38 must be a prime number too." Can you explain why David has made a mistake?

_____

_____

_____

Brain-buster Find the highest factor that is shared by 96 and 150.

_____

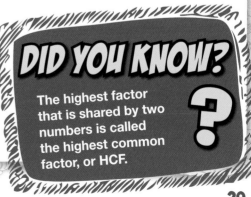

DID YOU KNOW?

The highest factor that is shared by two numbers is called the highest common factor, or HCF.

Simplifying fractions

One half is one out of two equal parts!

↻ Recap

Fractions show proportions of a whole.

They have a **numerator** on the top, and a **denominator** on the bottom.

numerator ⟶ $\dfrac{1}{2}$ ⟵ denominator

📄 Revise

We usually simplify fractions to make them easier to understand.

$\frac{250}{500}$ is the same as $\frac{1}{2}$

It's obvious which one is easier to read and understand.

To simplify fractions you must understand factors.

Look at the dots below.

These statements are true:

   Three out of 12 are red.
   One in every four is red.

So, $\frac{3}{12}$ is the same as $\frac{1}{4}$.

We say that the fraction has been **simplified**.

We can also simplify fractions using common factors.

To simplify $\frac{24}{30}$ we can separate each number into suitable factor pairs:

Factors of 24 = 1 × 24, 2 × 12, 3 × 8, 4 × 6

Factors of 30 = 1 × 30, 2 × 15, 3 × 10, 5 × 6

Six is the highest common factor of both 24 and 30. Therefore...

$$\frac{24}{30} = \frac{4 \times 6}{5 \times 6}$$

$$\frac{24 \div 6}{30 \div 6} = \frac{4}{5}$$

💡 Tips

Simple tips for simplifying fractions!

- If you can't spot the highest common factor, look for a lower common factor for the numerator and the denominator and divide the numerator and the denominator to simplify and keep going until you get to the smallest number for example:

$$\frac{18 \div 2}{48 \div 2} = \frac{9 \div 3}{24 \div 3} = \frac{3}{8}$$ Or, just divide 18 and 48 by 6!

Talk maths

The player with the most correct **bings**, **bangs** and **bongs** wins the game!

Play *Big Bang Bong*.

Any number of people can play. You will each need a pencil and paper.

Take turns to call out a fraction (such as, twelve fifteenths). Everyone must write down the fraction in numerator and denominator form, and then it is a race to simplify the fraction as much as possible.

The first person to simplify the fraction must shout bing! Everyone must then agree that they are right.

If they have made a mistake, the first person to spot and correct it shouts bang!

If a fraction has been suggested that cannot be simplified (such as seven sixteenths), the first person to realise this must shout bong!

✔ Check

1. **Write the highest common factor of each pair of numbers.**

   a. 6 and 10 = _____   **b.** 15 and 24 = _____   **c.** 45 and 17 = _____

   d. 100 and 40 = _____   **e.** 30 and 300 = _____   **f.** 11 and 88 = _____

2. **Say if these simplifications are true or false.**

   a. $\frac{43}{86} = \frac{1}{2}$ _____   **b.** $\frac{12}{60} = \frac{1}{5}$ _____   **c.** $\frac{21}{49} = \frac{3}{8}$ _____   **d.** $\frac{64}{100} = \frac{16}{25}$ _____

3. **Simplify these fractions.**

   a. $\frac{6}{8} =$ _____   **b.** $\frac{15}{20} =$ _____   **c.** $\frac{24}{32} =$ _____   **d.** $\frac{75}{100} =$ _____

   e. $\frac{36}{80} =$ _____   **f.** $\frac{45}{72} =$ _____   **g.** $\frac{128}{300} =$ _____   **h.** $\frac{64}{200} =$ _____

⚠ Problems

Brain-teaser 128 out of 400 children have school dinners.

Write this as a fraction in its simplest form. _____

Brain-buster What fraction of the children do not have school dinners?

Write the answer in its simplest form. _____

Comparing and ordering fractions

↻ Recap

We can compare and order fractions by giving them the same denominators. To do this we must understand **equivalent fractions**.

This rectangle has been cut into eight equal pieces, or eighths.

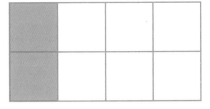

$\dfrac{2}{8} = \dfrac{1}{4}$ because we have divided the numerator and denominator by 2.

Two eighths is *equivalent* to one quarter because they are the same proportion of the whole.

We can check this by changing either one of them:

$$\dfrac{2 \div 2 = 1}{8 \div 2 = 4} \qquad\qquad \dfrac{1 \times 2 = 2}{4 \times 2 = 8}$$

> When simplifying a fraction, whatever you do to the numerator, you must do the same to the denominator.

▤ Revise

To compare and order fractions, we must give them the same denominator.

Which is bigger, $\frac{2}{5}$ or $\frac{1}{4}$?

We need to find the lowest common multiple which is 20 for 4 and 5, so we must convert each fraction into twentieths.

$$\dfrac{2 \times 4 = 8}{5 \times 4 = 20} \qquad\qquad \dfrac{1 \times 5 = 5}{4 \times 5 = 20} \qquad \text{So, } \tfrac{2}{5} \text{ is bigger than } \tfrac{1}{4}.$$

Let's try something harder. Which of these fractions is bigger, $\frac{7}{8}$ or $\frac{17}{20}$

The lowest common multiple for 8 and 20 is 40.

$$\dfrac{7 \times 5 = 35}{8 \times 5 = 40} \qquad\qquad \dfrac{17 \times 2 = 34}{20 \times 2 = 40} \qquad \text{So, } \tfrac{7}{8} \text{ is bigger than } \tfrac{17}{20}.$$

♀ Tips

- Remember, when we give each fraction the same denominator, it is called a **common denominator**.

- To compare any number of fractions, you need to give each fraction the same common denominator by finding the **lowest common multiple**. Look at page 28 if you are not certain.

- Remember, > means **is bigger than**, and < means **is smaller than**.

Talk maths

Try this with improper fractions, where the numerator is bigger. The same rules apply!

Write down a selection of fractions, making sure each one has a different numerator and denominator, such as $\frac{3}{7}$ $\frac{2}{3}$ $\frac{5}{8}$ $\frac{1}{9}$ $\frac{4}{6}$.

Next, choose any pair of fractions and change them to give them the same denominator. Then make a statement about them, such as:

$\frac{3}{7}$ and $\frac{2}{3}$ have a common denominator of 21.

$\frac{3}{7} = \frac{9}{21}$ and $\frac{2}{3} = \frac{14}{21}$ so $\frac{2}{3} > \frac{3}{7}$.

✔ Check

1. Change each fraction to give it a denominator of 30.

   a. $\frac{1}{2} =$ _____

   b. $\frac{2}{3} =$ _____

   c. $\frac{3}{5} =$ _____

   d. $\frac{5}{6} =$ _____

2. Insert the correct sign, =, < or >.

   a. $1\frac{1}{2}$ _____ $1\frac{3}{6}$

   b. $3\frac{3}{4}$ _____ $3\frac{2}{3}$

   c. $\frac{20}{6}$ _____ $\frac{13}{4}$

   d. $\frac{12}{5}$ _____ $\frac{15}{6}$

3. True or false?

   a. $\frac{3}{7} > \frac{1}{3}$ _____

   b. $\frac{15}{9} > \frac{7}{5}$ _____

   c. $\frac{7}{11} > \frac{13}{20}$ _____

4. Arrange these fractions in order, smallest to largest. Place a less than sign (<) between each one.

   a. $\frac{3}{4}, \frac{5}{8}, \frac{2}{3}$: _____

   b. $\frac{4}{9}, \frac{3}{7}, \frac{1}{3}$: _____

   c. $\frac{13}{24}, \frac{5}{9}, \frac{7}{12}$: _____

⚠ Problems

Brain-teaser Eva's mum has some money in her purse. She says that Eva can have a fraction of it. She offers Eva $\frac{3}{8}$ or $\frac{7}{20}$ of the money.

Which fraction will give Eva more money? _____

Brain-buster In a survey, some children were asked which pets they owned. $\frac{2}{7}$ of the children owned dogs and $\frac{3}{12}$ owned cats. The others owned no pets. Arrange the three sets of children in order, showing the fraction of each.

_____ < _____ < _____

Adding and subtracting fractions

↺ Recap

To add and subtract fractions, they must have the same denominator.

To add $\frac{1}{2}$ and $\frac{1}{3}$, first find the lowest common denominator ($2 \times 3 = 6$).

Next, convert each fraction to give it a denominator of 6.

$$\frac{1 \times 3 = 3}{2 \times 3 = 6} \qquad \frac{1 \times 2 = 2}{3 \times 2 = 6}$$

Then, add the new fractions:

$$\frac{3}{6} + \frac{2}{6} = \frac{5}{6}$$

> **And you must only add the numerators!**
> $\frac{3}{12} + \frac{4}{12} = \frac{7}{12}$

Taking away is exactly the same – you only subtract the numerators.

$$\frac{7}{10} - \frac{3}{10} = \frac{4}{10}$$

📋 Revise

The common denominator will usually be the lowest common multiple of all the fractions involved.

If one denominator is a multiple of the other, you only need to change one. For example:

$$\frac{3}{5} + \frac{1}{10} = \frac{6}{10} + \frac{1}{10} = \frac{7}{10}$$

Sometimes you will need to think more, for example:

$$\frac{3}{5} + \frac{1}{8} \qquad \text{40 is the lowest common multiple of 5 and 8.}$$

$$\frac{3}{5} = \frac{24}{40} \text{ and } \frac{1}{8} = \frac{5}{40}$$

💡 Tips

> **Here's how to add mixed numbers and improper fractions.**

- There are two ways to deal with improper fractions and mixed numbers.

  1. Add the whole numbers and the fractions separately.

  $$1\frac{1}{3} + 3\frac{5}{6}$$
  $$= 1 + 3 + \frac{1}{3} + \frac{5}{6}$$
  $$= 4 + \frac{2}{6} + \frac{5}{6}$$
  $$= 4\frac{7}{6} = 5\frac{1}{6}$$

  2. Use improper fractions.

  $$1\frac{1}{3} + 3\frac{5}{6}$$
  $$= \frac{4}{3} + \frac{23}{6}$$
  $$= \frac{8}{6} + \frac{23}{6}$$
  $$= \frac{31}{6} = 5\frac{1}{6}$$

  It works for subtraction too!

Talk maths

$$\frac{1}{2} \quad \frac{3}{4} \quad \frac{1}{3} \quad \frac{7}{12} \quad \frac{1}{6} \quad \frac{3}{10}$$

$$\frac{2}{3} \quad \frac{5}{9} \quad \frac{4}{5} \quad \frac{5}{8} \quad \frac{5}{6} \quad \frac{3}{4}$$

Work with a partner and challenge them to add and subtract fractions. You can *only* say fractions that have one denominator that is a multiple of the other. Use the fractions in the box, or make up some of your own, for example:

Add one third and five sixths

$$\left(\frac{1}{3} + \frac{5}{6} = \frac{2}{6} + \frac{5}{6} = \frac{7}{6} = 1\frac{1}{6}\right)$$

Challenge your partner to work it out then read their answer to you.

One third plus five sixths equals seven sixths, or one and one sixth.

✔ Check

1. Add these fractions.

a. $\frac{1}{6} + \frac{2}{3} =$ _____

b. $\frac{2}{5} + \frac{3}{10} =$ _____

c. $\frac{1}{4} + \frac{1}{8} + \frac{1}{2} =$ _____

2. Subtract these fractions.

a. $\frac{5}{8} - \frac{1}{2} =$ _____

b. $\frac{7}{9} - \frac{1}{3} =$ _____

c. $\frac{7}{12} - \frac{2}{5} =$ _____

3. Insert the missing sign (+ or –).

a. $\frac{1}{2} \underline{\quad} \frac{1}{4} = \frac{3}{4}$

b. $\frac{1}{2} \underline{\quad} \frac{1}{3} = \frac{1}{6}$

c. $\frac{1}{2} \underline{\quad} \frac{2}{5} = \frac{9}{10}$

d. $\frac{2}{7} \underline{\quad} \frac{1}{6} = \frac{5}{42}$

e. $\frac{7}{10} \underline{\quad} \frac{1}{4} = \frac{9}{20}$

f. $\frac{3}{8} \underline{\quad} \frac{1}{12} = \frac{11}{24}$

4. Complete these calculations.

a. $\frac{5}{2} + \frac{7}{4} =$ _____

b. $2\frac{1}{2} - 1\frac{1}{4} =$ _____

c. $\frac{10}{3} - \frac{11}{5} =$ _____

d. $2\frac{2}{3} + 1\frac{4}{5} =$ _____

⚠ Problems

Brain-teaser Emma and Tom buy a pizza. If Emma eats $\frac{1}{2}$ of it and Tom eats $\frac{1}{3}$,

how much pizza is left over? _____

Brain-buster Richard and Amy have some popcorn. Richard eats three sevenths of it and Amy eats four elevenths of it.

How much popcorn is left? _____

Multiplying fractions

Remember, multiplication works in any order: $\frac{1}{2} \times 24$ is the same as $24 \times \frac{1}{2}$.

↻ Recap

We can multiply whole numbers by fractions.

When multiplying by a fraction we use the word **of**.

- $\frac{1}{2}$ of 10 = 5.
- One quarter of 12 is 3.
- $\frac{1}{3}$ of 9 is 3.

Revise

We can also multiply fractions by other fractions.

Watch carefully: when we multiply fractions together we multiply the numerators with each other *and* we multiply the denominators with each other.

$$\frac{1}{2} \times \frac{3}{4} = \frac{1 \times 3}{2 \times 4} = \frac{3}{8}$$

Look at the circle opposite. Can you see how half of three quarters equals three-eighths?

Let's try something harder:

$$\frac{5}{6} \times \frac{2}{3} = \frac{5 \times 2}{6 \times 3} = \frac{10}{18}$$ (we can simplify this to $\frac{5}{9}$)

$\frac{3}{4}$

All whole numbers can be written as fractions with a denominator of 1.

So, $5 \times \frac{3}{8}$ is the same as saying $\frac{5}{1} \times \frac{3}{8} = \frac{15}{8}$ (or $1\frac{7}{8}$).

Tips

This trick might save you time, but only use it if you understand it!

- Look at this calculation: $$\frac{2}{3} \times \frac{3}{5} = \frac{2 \times 3}{3 \times 5} = \frac{6}{15} = \frac{2}{5}$$

We didn't really need to do a calculation because the three on the top cancels out with the three on the bottom (3 ÷ 3 = 1).

- Can you see the quick way to solve this calculation?

$$\frac{3}{7} \times \frac{7}{9} = \frac{3 \times 7}{7 \times 9} = \frac{3}{9} = \frac{1}{3}$$

- Remember to simplify fractions as much as possible.

💬 Talk maths

Choose any two fractions from the examples in the box. Read them aloud as a multiplication. Try solving the problem mentally, explaining your answer.

$$\frac{7}{10} \quad \frac{5}{8} \quad \frac{5}{6} \quad \frac{2}{7} \quad \frac{4}{5} \quad \frac{1}{4} \quad \frac{2}{3} \quad \frac{1}{2}$$

$\frac{7}{10} \times \frac{4}{5} = \frac{28}{50}$ because **7 × 4 = 28**, and **10 × 5 = 50**.

Also, 2 is a common factor of 28 and 50, so we can simplify to $\frac{14}{25}$.

✔ Check

1. Complete these multiplications.

   a. $\frac{1}{2}$ of 20 = _____

   b. $\frac{1}{4}$ of 24 = _____

   c. $\frac{3}{4}$ of 24 = _____

   d. $\frac{2}{5} \times 25$ = _____

   e. $\frac{5}{6}$ of 30 = _____

   f. $\frac{2}{3} \times 39$ = _____

2. Write these answers as mixed numbers.

   a. $14 \times \frac{1}{4}$ = _____

   b. $25 \times \frac{1}{2}$ = _____

   c. $40 \times \frac{1}{3}$ = _____

   d. $14 \times \frac{3}{7}$ = _____

   e. $12 \times \frac{3}{5}$ = _____

   f. $100 \times \frac{1}{6}$ = _____

3. Multiply these fractions.

   a. $\frac{1}{2} \times \frac{1}{3}$ = _____

   b. $\frac{2}{5} \times \frac{3}{4}$ = _____

   c. $\frac{3}{8} \times \frac{8}{9}$ = _____

   d. $\frac{5}{6} \times \frac{4}{5}$ = _____

   e. $\frac{2}{3} \times \frac{5}{8}$ = _____

   f. $\frac{10}{7} \times \frac{4}{5}$ = _____

⚠ Problems

Brain-teaser Tinashe usually takes ten and a half minutes to run one lap of the park. In her roller skates she can do the same lap in half this time. How long will it take her in roller skates?

_____

Brain-buster A second is $\frac{1}{60}$ of a minute, and a minute is $\frac{1}{60}$ of an hour.

What is a second as a fraction of an hour? _____

Dividing fractions

↺ Recap

When multiplying by a fraction we multiply the numerators together, and we multiply the denominators together.

$$\frac{1}{5} \times \frac{3}{4} = \frac{1 \times 3}{5 \times 4} = \frac{3}{20}$$

Revise

Just as we can multiply fractions, we can also divide fractions. Look at the circle opposite. Half has been shaded.

If we divide the shaded half in two we get quarters.

So: $\frac{1}{2} \div 2 = \frac{1}{4}$.

Remember $\frac{1}{2} \div \frac{1}{2} = \frac{1}{4}$. So, dividing by 2 is the same as multiplying by $\frac{1}{2}$.

Now try this one: $\frac{1}{4} \div 3$

This is the same as saying $\frac{1}{4} \div \frac{1}{3} = \frac{1}{12}$.

Try drawing a circle and dividing it into fractions to prove this.

💡 Tips

- Dividing fractions is tricky.
  But remember that dividing by a whole number is the same as multiplying by one over that number, such as:

  $\frac{2}{3} \div 5$ is the same as $\frac{2}{3} \div \frac{5}{1}$ which is the same as $\frac{2}{3} \times \frac{1}{5} = \frac{2}{15}$.

  So, $\frac{2}{3} \div 5 = \frac{2}{15}$.

Talk maths

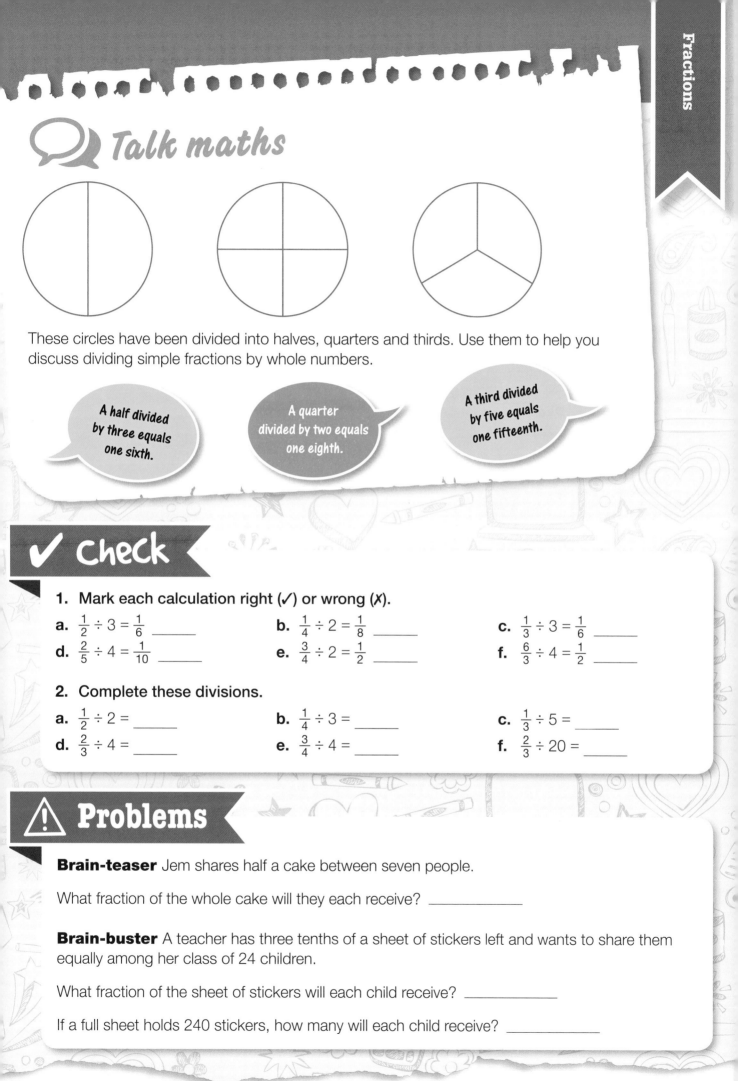

These circles have been divided into halves, quarters and thirds. Use them to help you discuss dividing simple fractions by whole numbers.

A half divided by three equals one sixth.

A quarter divided by two equals one eighth.

A third divided by five equals one fifteenth.

✔ Check

1. Mark each calculation right (✓) or wrong (✗).

a. $\frac{1}{2} \div 3 = \frac{1}{6}$ _____

b. $\frac{1}{4} \div 2 = \frac{1}{8}$ _____

c. $\frac{1}{3} \div 3 = \frac{1}{6}$ _____

d. $\frac{2}{5} \div 4 = \frac{1}{10}$ _____

e. $\frac{3}{4} \div 2 = \frac{1}{2}$ _____

f. $\frac{6}{3} \div 4 = \frac{1}{2}$ _____

2. Complete these divisions.

a. $\frac{1}{2} \div 2 =$ _____

b. $\frac{1}{4} \div 3 =$ _____

c. $\frac{1}{3} \div 5 =$ _____

d. $\frac{2}{3} \div 4 =$ _____

e. $\frac{3}{4} \div 4 =$ _____

f. $\frac{2}{3} \div 20 =$ _____

⚠ Problems

Brain-teaser Jem shares half a cake between seven people.

What fraction of the whole cake will they each receive? _____

Brain-buster A teacher has three tenths of a sheet of stickers left and wants to share them equally among her class of 24 children.

What fraction of the sheet of stickers will each child receive? _____

If a full sheet holds 240 stickers, how many will each child receive? _____

Decimal equivalents

↻ Recap

A proper fraction is a proportion of one whole.

$$\frac{1}{4}, \frac{1}{3}, \frac{1}{2}, \frac{2}{3}, \frac{3}{4}$$ are all proper fractions.

A fraction is a numerator divided by a denominator, such as:

$\frac{1}{2}$ is 1 divided by 2, so $\frac{1}{2} = 0.5$

You need to learn these common fractions and their decimal equivalents:

Fraction	$\frac{1}{2}$	$\frac{1}{4}$	$\frac{3}{4}$	$\frac{1}{5}$	$\frac{1}{10}$
Decimal	0.5	0.25	0.75	0.2	0.1

Revise

Any fraction can be written as a decimal.
If you need to calculate the decimal equivalent of a fraction, just do a short division.

$$\frac{1}{4} = \begin{array}{r} 0\ .\ 2\ \ 5 \\ 4\overline{\smash{\big)}\ 1\ .\ {}^1 0\ {}^2 0} \end{array}$$

Notice that a whole number can be written with zeros in the decimal places.

$$\frac{3}{8} = \begin{array}{r} 0\ .\ 3\ \ 7\ \ 5 \\ 8\overline{\smash{\big)}\ 3\ .\ {}^3 0\ {}^6 0\ {}^4 0} \end{array}$$

Remember to keep the decimal point in the right place!

Tips

Time for some decimal tips!

- Remember that, after a decimal point, the first column is tenths, the second column is hundredths, and the third column is thousandths.

- We read decimals aloud using the numbers zero to nine.
  We say 0.5 is **zero point five**.
  We say 0.75 is **zero point seven five**.
  We say 0.375 is **zero point three seven five**.
  We say 0.666 is **zero point six six six**.

Talk maths

You know about fraction equivalents, such as $\frac{2}{4} = \frac{1}{2}$.

Now look at what happens when they are changed to decimals.

$$\frac{2}{4} = 0.5 \qquad \frac{1}{2} = 0.5$$

Discuss this with an adult, completing this chart as you go.

Fraction	$\frac{2}{8} = \frac{1}{4}$	$\frac{4}{10} = \frac{2}{5}$	$\frac{2}{6} = \frac{1}{3}$	$\frac{6}{8} = \frac{3}{4}$	$\frac{10}{12} = \frac{5}{6}$
Decimal	0.25	0.4			

✔ Check

1. Convert these fractions to decimals.

   a. $\frac{2}{5}$ = _____

   b. $\frac{6}{10}$ = _____

   c. $\frac{3}{8}$ = _____

2. Complete this chart.

Fraction	$\frac{1}{8}$	$\frac{2}{8}$	$\frac{3}{8}$	$\frac{4}{8}$	$\frac{5}{8}$	$\frac{6}{8}$	$\frac{7}{8}$	$\frac{8}{8}$
Decimal	0.125	0.25						

3. Match each fraction to its decimal equivalent.

   $\frac{3}{4}$ $\quad$ $\frac{5}{8}$ $\quad$ $\frac{4}{5}$ $\quad$ $\frac{1}{3}$

   0.625 $\quad$ 0.8 $\quad$ 0.333 $\quad$ 0.75

4. Match each decimal to its fraction equivalent.

   0.166 $\quad$ 0.4 $\quad$ 0.7 $\quad$ 0.125

   $\frac{1}{8}$ $\quad$ $\frac{1}{6}$ $\quad$ $\frac{7}{10}$ $\quad$ $\frac{2}{5}$

⚠ Problems

Brain-teaser Which is more, $\frac{5}{6}$ or 0.8? _____

Brain-buster A bag of popcorn is shared equally between 12 people. Tim says that each person will receive 0.1 of the popcorn. Is he right? Explain your answer.

_____

_____

Decimal places

A decimal fraction has 10, 100 or 1000 as its denominator, such as $\frac{4}{10}$.

We can say $\frac{4}{10}$ as 4 divided by 10.

When we divide a number by 10, 100 or 1000, we move the numbers to the right.

Fraction name	Fraction	Decimal	Decimal name
seven tenths	$\frac{7}{10}$	0.7	Zero point seven
twenty three hundredths	$\frac{23}{100}$	0.23	Zero point two three
four hundred and thirty five thousandths	$\frac{435}{1000}$	0.435	Zero point four three five

> The place value of each digit changes.

📋 Revise

> Money usually needs to be rounded to two decimal places.

Decimals can have more than three decimal places, but usually we round decimals, just like we round other numbers.

A basic rule for rounding is if the next number is five or more, round up, if not, round down.

0.87 = 0.9 to one decimal place

0.435 = 0.44 to two decimal places

0.2574 = 0.257 to three decimal places

Look at these examples.

Fraction	$\frac{1}{7}$	$\frac{7}{17}$
Decimal	0.142857	0.411764
Rounded to three decimal places	0.143	0.412
Rounded to two decimal places	0.14	0.41
Rounded to one decimal place	0.1	0.4

💡 Tips

- Some decimals have the same number that goes on forever, such as

$\frac{1}{6}$ = 0.16666666666666666666 6666666666666666666

We call this a recurring decimal. We usually round these decimals to three decimal places.

So $\frac{1}{6}$ = 0.167 to three decimal places.

- $\frac{1}{3}$ and $\frac{2}{3}$ also make recurring decimals.

- $\frac{1}{3}$ = 0.333 to three decimal places. $\frac{2}{3}$ = 0.667 to three decimal places.

Talk maths

You will need two or more people.

Think of a fraction with demoninators of 2, 4, 5 or 8 and then use division to calculate the decimal equivalent.

$\frac{2}{5} = 0.4$

Take turns to challenge each other to say the decimal to one, two or three decimal places, checking each other's answers.

✔ Check

1. Look at these decimals and say how many thousandths, hundredths and tenths each one has.

   a. 0.375 _____ thousandths _____ hundredths _____ tenths

   b. 0.903 _____ thousandths _____ hundredths _____ tenths

2. Complete this chart.

Fraction	Decimal	Rounded to three decimal places	Rounded to two decimal places	Rounded to one decimal place
$\frac{2}{7}$	0.285714			
$\frac{3}{13}$	0.230769			
$\frac{4}{11}$	0.363636			
$\frac{2}{3}$	0.666667			
$\frac{8}{9}$	0.888889			

⚠ Problems

Brain-teaser Jared says that 0.001 rounded to the nearest tenth is 0.1. Is he right? _____

Explain your answer. _____

Brain-buster Explain why $\frac{3}{11}$ is a recurring number, and round it to three decimal places.

_____

Multiplying decimals

↻ Recap

Do you remember what tenths, hundredths and thousands are?
Tenths are bigger than hundredths, and hundredths are bigger than thousandths.

| 0.6 > 0.5 | 0.431 > 0.429 | 0.1 > 0.099 | 0.3 > 0.28 | 0.515 > 0.4 |

- There are ten tenths in a whole.
- There are one hundred hundredths in a whole, but ten hundredths in one tenth.
- There are one thousand thousandths in a whole, but ten thousandths in one hundredth.

one hundred and twenty-three thousandths
= zero point one two three
$\frac{123}{1000} = 0.123$

Ones	Tenths	Hundredths	Thousandths
0 .	1	2	3

📄 Revise

We can multiply any two numbers together, including numbers that are decimals.
For the moment, we will learn how to multiply a decimal by a whole number.
This will come in very handy for solving money problems!

Do you remember how to use formal written methods for multiplication?

```
    3  2  4
×      1  3
    9  7¹ 2
 3  2  4  0  +
 4  2  1  2
```
Answer: 4212

Well, the same method works for decimals.

```
    4 · 1  3
×      2  3
 1  2 . 3  9
 8  2 . 6  0  +
 9  4 · 9  9
```
Answer: 94.99

> It's all about place value. Just remember to keep the decimal point in the right place.

💡 Tips

- When you multiply a decimal by a whole number, make sure you give your answer as a decimal too, with the same number of decimal places, for example:
  6.35 × 2 = 12.70 or £1.25 × 4 = £5.00
  Keeping the zeros helps with checking work later on.

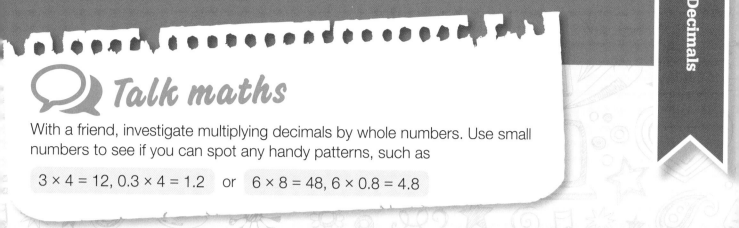

Talk maths

With a friend, investigate multiplying decimals by whole numbers. Use small numbers to see if you can spot any handy patterns, such as

3 × 4 = 12, 0.3 × 4 = 1.2   or   6 × 8 = 48, 6 × 0.8 = 4.8

✔ Check

1. Complete each of these decimal multiplications using a written method.

a.
	0 . 2
×	3

b.
	3 . 3
×	2

c.
	0 . 2 3
×	4

d.
	0 . 3 4
×	6

2. Complete each of these long divisions using a written method.

a. 0.23 × 21

b. 0.45 × 15

c. 0.25 × 25

d. 3.33 × 33

⚠ Problems

Brain-teaser A group of eight friends decide to buy their teacher some flowers.

If they each contribute £1.15, how much will they have? _____

Brain-buster A school trip is going to cost exactly £100. A letter is sent home asking for a donation of £2.65 per child towards the trip. If there are 32 children in the class and they all make the contribution, how much more will the school have to contribute?

_____

Dividing decimals

↺ Recap

Short division

	0	4	2	6	r2
8	3	³4	²1	⁵0	

In short division we carry on the remainder at each stage, but with long division we calculate the remainder at each stage, so that there is less chance of errors.

Long division

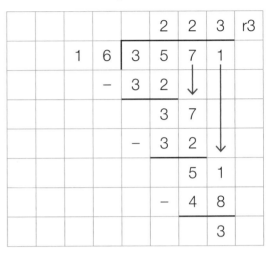

					2	2	3	r3
		1	6	3	5	7	1	
		−		3	2	↓		
					3	7		
		−			3	2	↓	
						5	1	
		−				4	8	
							3	

目 Revise

We can use short and long division for dividing decimals.
Just remember to keep the decimal point in the same place.

	0 .	8	7
4	3 .	³4	²8

				1 .	6	4
	1	3	2	1 .	3	2
(13 × 1 →)	−	1	3	↓		
			8	3		
(13 × 6 →)	−	7	8	↓		
			5	2		
(13 × 4 →)	−	5	2			
			0	0		

✔ Check

1. Complete each of these short divisions of decimals.

a.

3	0 .	3	9

b.

2	0 .	5	4

c.

4	0 .	9	6

2. On paper, complete these long divisions of decimals using a written method.

   a. 0.6 ÷ 15   b. 7.04 ÷ 32
   c. 3.30 ÷ 22   d. 77.4 ÷ 15

⚠ Problems

Brain-teaser Aysha has a brother and a sister. Their mum gives them £10.44 pocket money, to share equally between the three of them. How much will they each get?

_____

Percentage equivalents

Decimal fractions can be called percentages.

↻ Recap

$\frac{65}{100}$ is a decimal fraction.

We can say **65 over 100** or **65 out of 100**.

Per cent means **parts of a hundred** or **out of 100**. Look at the 100 grid. 65 out of the 100 squares are shaded, this is 65%.

$0.65 = \frac{65}{100} = 65\%$

📄 Revise

It is easy to find the equivalents of simple fractions and decimals.

We can use our knowledge of decimal places and rounding to help us find trickier equivalents.

Fraction	$\frac{1}{2}$	$\frac{1}{4}$	$\frac{1}{10}$	$\frac{1}{5}$	$\frac{3}{4}$	$\frac{1}{1}$
Decimal	0.5	0.25	0.1	0.2	0.75	1.0
Per cent	50%	25%	10%	20%	75%	100%

$\frac{3}{8} = 0.375 = 37.5\%$ $\frac{5}{6} = 0.833 = 83.3\%$

✔ Check

1. Complete the chart.

Percentage	Decimal	Fraction
33.3%		
	0.125	
		$\frac{2}{5}$
	0.85	
		$\frac{7}{8}$

⚠ Problems

Brain-teaser 12 out of 30 children have blond hair. What is that as a percentage? _____

Ratio and proportion: numbers

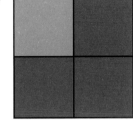

And, of course, three out of four of the squares are red.

↻ Recap

A fraction shows us one number compared to a whole.
In the shape opposite, one out of four of the squares is blue.

Proportion is the fraction of a whole.
For this shape, the proportion of blue squares is one in four, or one out of four. And the proportion of red squares is three in four, or three out of four.

Ratio is different, because it compares amounts.
For the shape above, the ratio of blue squares to red squares is 1 to 3, or 1:3.

Revise

Look at these examples.

In total there are 100 animals on a farm.
There are two dogs, three cats, five rabbits, 20 cows, 30 sheep and 40 chickens.

Proportion

The proportion of dogs is two out of 100 animals. As a fraction this is $\frac{2}{100}$ or $\frac{1}{50}$.

The proportion of rabbits is $\frac{5}{100}$ or $\frac{1}{20}$.
One in every 20 animals is a rabbit.

Ratio

The ratio of dogs to cows is 2:20.
This can be simplified to 1:10.
There are ten cows for every dog.

The ratio of cows to chickens is 20:40.
This can be simplified to 1:2.
For every cow there are two chickens.

Tips

- Proportion is a fraction of the whole; ratio compares different amounts.
- One in every five adults play computer games (so four out of five do not play).
  As a *proportion* this is one out of five, or $\frac{1}{5}$.
  But the *ratio* of adults who do play to adults who don't play computer games is 1:4.

Talk maths

A wall is covered with 100 tiles.

Ten are black, 20 are white, 15 are red, 15 are yellow and 40 are blue.

Work with a friend to agree on some proportion and ratio statements about the tiles.

Remember to write the ratio in the simplest form.

✔ Check

1. **Write the proportion of black squares in each pattern.**

a. _____   b. _____   c. _____

2. **Look at this pattern and write the ratios.**

a. Blue to red ____ : ____   b. Red to green ____ : ____   c. Yellow to green ____ : ____

⚠ Problems

Brain-teaser In a class of 30 pupils, six of the class can speak two languages.

a. What proportion of the class can speak two languages? _____

b. What is the ratio of dual-language to single-language speakers? _____

Brain-buster A recipe for a fruit pie says to add blackberries and blueberries in the ratio 3:4.

a. If Hana has 15 blackberries, how many blueberries will she need? _____

b. What proportion of the berries will be blueberries? _____

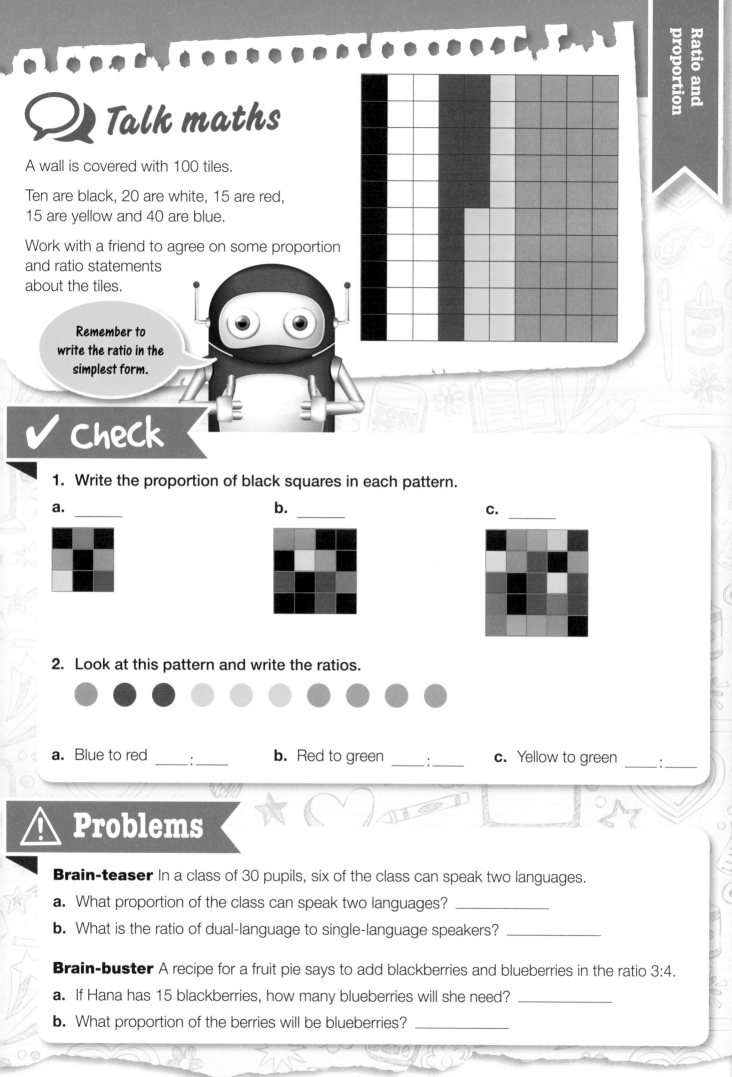

Ratio and proportion: percentages

↻ Recap

> And the proportion of green triangles is 2 in 3, or 2 out of 3.

Proportion is the fraction of a whole. For this shape, the proportion of yellow triangles is one in three, or one out of three.

Ratio compares amounts. For this shape, the ratio of yellow to green triangles is one to two, or 1:2.

> And the ratio of *green to yellow* triangles is two to one or 2:1.

📄 Revise

> That's easy. What if there were only 50 children?

Percentages are a type of proportion. They represent an amount out of 100.

35 children **out of 100** have packed lunches, which is $\frac{35}{100}$ or 35%.

If 17 children out of 50 have brown eyes, as a proportion it is $\frac{17}{50}$.

Percentages must be out of 100, so we must adjust the fraction.

$\frac{17}{50} = \frac{34}{100}$ so 34% have brown eyes.

Remember that 100% is everything, so, if 34% of the children have brown eyes, 66% do not, because 34% + 66% = 100%.

💡 Tips

- When calculating percentages, choose the order of calculations you find easier, for example, to find 26% of 360:

  - You can either find 25% ($\frac{1}{4}$) of 360 = 90, plus 1% of 360 = 3.6.

    $360 \times 25 = 90$ **plus** $360 \div 1 = 3.6$
    or $90 + 3.6 = 93.6$

  - Or you can do 26 × 360, then divide by 100.

    $26 \times 360 = 9360$
    $9360 \div 100 = 93.6$

💬 Talk maths

You will need a pack of playing cards with the picture cards removed.
This will leave 40 cards, 1–10 in each suit of clubs, diamonds, spades and hearts.

Sort the pack in different ways and then make statements of proportion, ratio and percentage, such as:
One in four cards is a diamond.
The ratio of diamonds to other cards is 1:3.
25% of the pack is diamonds.

DID YOU KNOW?

1 in 40 is 2.5%

✔ Check

1. Write these proportions as a percentage.

   a. 1 in 4 = _____   **b.** 7 in 10 = _____   **c.** 2 in 5 = _____   **d.** 3 in 8 = _____

2. Write these percentages as a proportion in their simpliest form.

   a. 25% = _____   **b.** 40% = _____   **c.** 26% = _____   **d.** 87.5% = _____

3. Calculate these percentages.

   a. 25% of 200 = _____   **b.** 50% of 1 = _____   **c.** 10% of 624 = _____

   d. 95% of 300 = _____   **e.** 60% of 24 = _____   **f.** 15% of 360 = _____

4. Explain what each of these mathematical terms mean.
   a. Percentage: _____
   b. Proportion: _____
   c. Ratio: _____

⚠ Problems

Brain-teaser In a traffic survey, children counted 220 cars. 25% were driving over the speed limit.

How many cars were driving too fast? _____

Brain-buster The percentage of homes in the UK where a dog is kept as a pet is 18%.

If there are 42 million homes in total, how many of these will keep a dog? _____

Scale factors

And the ratio of yellow to red beads is five to one, or 5:1.

↻ Recap

Ratio compares amounts.
For every red bead there are five yellow beads.
The ratio of red to yellow beads is 1:5.

📝 Revise

People often draw to scale. This means changing the proportion of what is drawn.

We have to draw things to scale to fit our drawings on the paper!

Scale is usually shown as a ratio.
The brown line is four times longer than the green line.
The scale of **green:brown** is **1:4**.

Jez is 125cm tall.
His brother draws a picture of her using a scale of 1:10.
His drawing will be 12.5cm tall.

The scale of this map is 1:100,000.
Every 1cm on the map represents 100,000cm (or 1km) in real life.

B6457

A18

SCALE: 1 : 100,000

0   1000   2000   3000   4000

💡 Tips

Scaling up and down is easy when you follow my tips!

- Remember that scale can work the other way round too. If you want to draw an insect, it's easier to enlarge it. So, if an ant is 3mm long an enlargement of 50:1 would give a drawing of 50 × 3 = 150mm, or 15cm.

3mm

💬 Talk maths

Or just draw their hand – remember to measure it before you start.

You will need a sheet of paper, a pencil and a ruler. Measure these objects, and then try to draw an enlargement of each object, using a scale of 5:1. Take your drawings and explain them to an adult. To finish, try a friend or an adult at a scale of 1:10.

✔ check

1. **This line is 4cm long.**

    How long would these enlargements be?

    a. 2:1 _____   **b.** 5:1 _____   **c.** 10:1 _____

2. **This square has a side of 1cm.**

    Complete this chart for different scale enlargements.

Scale of enlargement	Side length	Area
5:1		
10:1		
25:1		

3. **A table is 1m high.**

    What height would models be if they were made to these scales?

    a. 1:2 _____   **b.** 1:5 _____   **c.** 1:20 _____

⚠ Problems

Brain-teaser A model of a house is made to a scale of 1:25.

If the model is 22cm high, what height is the actual house? _____

Brain-buster Anita makes a sculpture of a mouse. The actual mouse is 8cm high. The sculpture is 60cm high.

What is the scale of the enlargement? _____

Using simple formulae

↻ Recap

If we need to calculate the perimeter or area of a regular shape, we can use a formula.

For the rectangle, we can say,
Area equals length multiplied by width.
In a formula, we can use a letter for each part.
So, **area equals length multiplied by width** becomes $A = l \times w$.

A = area   *l* = length   *w* = width

←—— Length (*l*) ——→

Width (*w*)

▤ Revise

←—— Length 4cm ——→

Width 3cm

In formulae, we can drop the multiplication sign. If a letter and a number, or two letters, are together, it means that they are being multiplied.

The area of a rectangle is $A = lw$.
For the red rectangle, $A = 4 \times 3 = 12cm^2$

For a rectangle that is 7m long and 2m wide: $A = 7 \times 2 = 14m^2$.
For a rectangular field that is 90m long and 30m wide:
$A = 90 \times 30 = 2700m^2$.

Notice that area has square units. It is shown with this symbol ^{2}.

Perimeter is the distance around a shape.
For a rectangle $P = l + w + l + w$ or, $P = 2l + 2w$.
Remember, multiplication before addition.
For the red rectangle, $P = 2 \times 4 + 2 \times 3 = 14cm$.

You can use other formulas in the same way. Just replace the letters with the numbers.

The great thing about a formula is that you can use it again and again. The letters always stay the same but they represent different numbers.

💡 Tips

- Be sure to get your units right. Formulae are used to calculate all sorts of things: distance, area, temperature, weight, volume, and so on. You must be sure to keep everything in the same units.

- If you are calculating with different units, you must convert one unit to the other first: you must multiply centimetre by centimetre, add grams to grams, and so on.

Talk maths

Try inventing your own simple formulae, and then test them on an adult, for example:

- Some new houses are being built.
  If every house has seven windows, a formula for windows is:
  $w = 7h$, where h = the number of houses, and w = the number of windows.
- How about cars? You need five tyres per car.
- Or currant buns? There are 24 currants per bun!

If there are six houses there must be 42 windows!

If there are 100 houses, there will be 700 windows!

✓ Check

1. Complete the chart for perimeters and areas of rectangles.

Length	Width	Perimeter	Area
5cm	2cm		
5m	4m		
7km	1.5km		
3.2m	2.3m		

2. Use this formula to complete the chart:
   $h = 3f + 8$

h					
f	1	2	4	9	100

⚠ Problems

Brain-teaser Beth wants to change some pounds to dollars. The formula for calculating the amount of pounds she receives is $ = 1.67 × £. £ is the amount of pounds Beth has and $ is the dollars she will receive. (1.67 is called the exchange rate.)

If Beth has £200 to change, how many dollars will she receive? _____

Brain-buster Here is the formula for changing degrees Fahrenheit to degrees Celsius:

$C = \frac{5}{9} × (F - 32)$

Use the formula to complete this chart.

°C °F
+10 — 50
0 — 32
−10 — 14

Fahrenheit	32°	104°	212°
Celsius			

Missing numbers

↺ Recap

Sometimes equations have missing numbers.

4 +  = 12

Easy! The missing number is 8.

4.3 − ● = 3.1

Not so easy! The missing number is...1.2.

📄 Revise

For harder problems, it can help to put a letter in the place of the missing number.

● − 9 = 23

$h - 9 = 23$

$h - 9 + 9 = 23 + 9$

$h = 32$

Now try this one: 3 × ● = 30

And this one: 4 + 2 × ● = 30

Because the equation must balance, you must add the same amount to each side of the equals sign. Look...

💡 Tips

• Don't forget that missing numbers could be negative numbers or decimals. Can you see the answers for these two?

● + 3 = 2

(missing number = −1)

3.1 + ● = 7.5

(missing number = 4.4)

The numbers might be missing, but the tip isn't...

DID YOU KNOW?

An equation must always balance, like scales. Everything on one side of the equals sign must equal everything on the other side.

Talk maths

> There is something so satisfying about confusing an adult!

Test an adult with some missing numbers.
Secretly write a calculation nice and large, and make sure that you have the right answer, for example:

$$13 - 3 \times 4 = 1$$

Cover any one of the numbers with your finger, and challenge them to calculate the hidden number.

✔ Check

1. Insert the missing numbers to make these equations true.

a. $23 - \bigcirc = 15$ **b.** $\bigcirc - 7 = 11$ **c.** $6 + \bigcirc = 31$ **d.** $\bigcirc + 13 = 11$

e. $4 \times \bigcirc = 24$ **f.** $49 \div \bigcirc = 7$ **g.** $23 + 4 \times \bigcirc = 39$ **h.** $\bigcirc \div 3 - 4 = 7$

2. Solve these problems.

a. $45 = \bigcirc - 17$ **b.** $23 = 11 + 2 \times \bigcirc$ **c.** $7.3 = \bigcirc - 2.7$ **d.** $6 = \bigcirc + 9$

⚠ Problems

Brain-teaser A teacher has been collecting dinner money, but she dropped some of her own money into the bowl by accident. She knows that 25 children each gave her £1.50, and that there is £42.50 in the bowl.

Write an equation for the missing money, and use it to find out how much money the teacher should take back.

_____

Brain-buster Some children are raising money for charity. They *each* raise £5.60.
An anonymous donor says that they will match the amount raised.
The total amount raised, including the donation, is £190.40.

Write an equation for the money, and use it to find out how many children took part.

_____

Equations with two unknowns

↺ Recap

Algebra uses letters as well as numbers. Letters are sometimes referred to as **variables**, or **unknowns**. The letters **represent** numbers.

We can solve an equation to find the value of an **unknown** number. $16 - a = 7$

We can move letters and numbers around, but we must keep the calculation balanced.

Whatever we do to one side, we must do to the other!

How to find a:

$16 - a = 7$

$16 = 7 + a$ (we added a to each side)

$9 = a$ (we took away 7 from each side)

$a = 9$ (we wrote the equation starting with '$a = ...$')

📋 Revise

DID YOU KNOW?

In real life scientists find equations like this very, very useful.

Equations can have more than one variable or unknown.

$x + y = 6$

The problem with equations that have two variables is that there can be more than one answer.

It goes on forever!

$x = 0, y = 6$	$x = 1, y = 5$	$x = 2, y = 4$
$x = 3, y = 3$	$x = 4, y = 2$	$x = 5, y = 1$
$x = 6, y = 0$	$x = 7, y = -1$	$x = -1, y = 7$

💡 Tips

- Spend time practising balancing equations with two unknowns. It will really help you to see how they work. These equations are all the same:

$p + q = 4$ $p = 4 - q$ $q = 4 - p$

Try putting $p = 3$ and $q = 1$ into each equation to check!

Talk maths

Start off by using small numbers only, but have a go with bigger ones too!

Working with a partner, choose one of the equations in the box and choose a variable each. The first person calls out a number for their letter, and the second person must find the value of the second variable.
Try it for all the equations.

$p = q + 4$

$a + b = 18$

$2x - y = 7$

$s + 3 = t - 4$

$23 - y = z$

✔ Check

1. Complete the table for each equation.

a. $y = x + 2$

x	0	1	2	3	4	5	−1	−2	−3
y									

b. $s + t = 8$

s	0	2	5	6	7	8	9	10	−1
t									

c. $p = 2q - 3$

q	0	1	1.5	2	5	10	100	−1	−10
p									

⚠ Problems

Brain-teaser Entry to the school disco is £2. The cost for disco hire is £120. The head teacher writes a formula to calculate the money they will raise.

$m = 2t - 120$

(m = the money they will make, and t = the number of tickets they will sell)

a. How many tickets must they sell to 'break even'? _____

b. How many tickets must they sell to make a profit of £50? _____

Break even means to lose nothing and gain nothing.

Brain-buster Rashid writes an equation $x^2 - y^2 = 32$. What numbers could he be thinking of if they are positive whole numbers?

What are the numbers he is thinking of? $x = $ _____ , $y = $ _____

Converting units

↺ Recap

Different quantities are measured in different ways.

Measure	Units of measurement	Abbreviations	
Time (years)	1 year = 12 months, = $365\frac{1}{4}$ days 1 year = approximately 52 weeks 1 week = 7 days	years = y months = m	weeks = w days = d
Time (days)	1 day = 24 hours 1 hour = 60 minutes 1 minute = 60 seconds	hours = h minutes = m	seconds = s
Length	1 kilometre = 1000 metres 1 metre = 100 centimetres 1 centimetre = 10 millimetres	kilometres = km metres = m	centimetres = cm millimetres = mm
Mass	1 kilogram = 1000 grams	kilograms = kg	grams = g
Capacity	1 litre = 100 centilitres 1 centilitre = 10 millilitres	litre = l centilitre = cl	millilitre = ml

🗐 Revise

Look at these conversion charts.

Converting length

Conversion	Operation	Example
mm to cm	÷ 10	12mm = 1.2cm
cm to m	÷ 100	256cm = 2.56m
m to km	÷ 1000	467m = 0.467km
cm to mm	× 10	3.5cm = 35mm
m to cm	× 100	1.85m = 185cm
km to m	× 1000	4.3km = 4300m

Converting mass

Conversion	Operation	Example
grams to kg	÷ 1000	250g = 0.25kg
kg to grams	× 1000	7.3kg = 7300g

Converting time

Conversion	Operation	Example
hours to days	÷ 24	48h = 2d
mins to hours	÷ 60	240m = 4h
seconds to mins	÷ 60	600s = 10m
days to hours	× 24	2d = 48h
hours to mins	× 60	7h = 420m
mins to seconds	× 60	10m = 600s

Converting capacity

Conversion	Operation	Example
cl to litres	÷ 100	7000cl = 70l
ml to litres	÷ 1000	3000ml = 3l
litres to cl	× 100	3l = 300cl
litres to ml	× 1000	2.3l = 2300ml

Tips

- You must always make sure that you are using the right units.
- To solve problems that have different quantities that can be measured, you may have to convert the units, such as 1kg + 340g = 1340g or 1.34kg

Talk maths

Work with an adult or a friend to practise converting units in your head. Using the charts on the page opposite, ask each other questions that you know will be possible to calculate mentally.

How many centimetres in 3m?

How many seconds in 5 minutes?

How many millilitres in 2.5l?

✔ Check

1. **Convert these times.**

   a. 5 hours into minutes _____

   b. 2 hours into seconds _____

   c. 510 seconds into minutes _____

   d. 1 day into seconds _____

2. **Convert these lengths.**

   a. 23m into millimetres _____

   b. 2.4km into metres _____

   c. 1km into centimetres _____

   d. 685mm into metres _____

3. **Convert these weights.**

   a. 750g into kilograms _____

   b. 32.5kg into grams _____

   c. 1g into kilograms _____

   d. 0.35kg into grams _____

4. **Convert these lengths.**

   a. 2.5l into millilitres _____

   b. 75cl into litres _____

   c. 63,425ml into litres _____

   d. 0.25l into millimetres _____

⚠ Problems

Brain-teaser The distance from Evie's front door to her school gate is exactly 242,637mm! How far is that in metres, centimetres and millimetres? (For example, 31,456mm is 31m, 45cm and 6mm.)

_____

Brain-buster How many seconds are there in a leap year? _____

Using measures

↻ Recap

Measures you should understand include:

Measure	Used for	Units
Capacity	Volumes of containers, quantities of liquid	1cl = 10ml 1l = 100cl 1l = 1000ml 1ml = 0.1cl 1ml = 0.001l
Length	Distances, lengths and areas	1km = 1000m 1m = 100cm 1cm = 10mm 1m = 0.001km 1cm = 0.01m 1mm = 0.1cm
Mass	Weights	1kg = 1000g 1g = 0.001kg
Time	Times, timetables, speed	1d = 24h 1h = 60m 1m = 60s

🗒 Revise

Arranging quantities with units in powers of 10 is called **metric**. Metric systems make conversion easy by multiplying or dividing by 10, 10^2 (100) or 10^3 (1000).

Remember, you can only add like units:

1.1l + 357ml = 1.457l or 1457ml

1.45km + 257m = 1.707km or 1707m

3.23m − 122.6cm = 2.004m or 200.4cm

0.24kg + 3245g = 3.485kg or 3485g

Time is a bit different. We give answers to time in hours, minutes and seconds.

45s + 25s = 70s = 1m 10s

40m + 50m = 90m = $1\frac{1}{2}$h

3h 50m − 100m = 2h 10m

Imperial units

We sometimes use imperial units for:

lengths

1 mile = 1760 yards

1 yard = 3 feet

1 foot = 12 inches

How many kilometres is ten miles?

1 inch = 2.54cm	1cm = 0.394 inches
1 mile = 1.61km	1km = 0.621 miles

weights

1 stone = 14 pounds (lb)

1lb = 16 ounces (oz)

1lb = 0.454kg	1kg = 2.205lb
1oz = 28.35g	1g = 0.035oz

capacity

1 gallon = 8 pints

1 pint = 0.57 litres	1 litre = 1.76 pints

💡 Tips

Metric or imperial? Learn both!

- We still have imperial units in daily life. In the past, everything was measured in imperial units. These are sometimes used in other countries, but in most of the world metric units are used. The key facts in the box above are worth learning by heart so that you can do quick mental conversions.

💬 Talk maths

You will need a tape measure, some scales and a measuring jug.

Working with an adult, look for a selection of different-sized objects from around the house. Discuss whether you will measure the length, weight or capacity of each object (for some objects you can measure more than one). Write down your estimates.

✔ Check

1. **Now find the actual measures of all your objects, using the appropriate equipment. With practice, you will find that your estimates become better and better.**

Object	Measure	Estimate	Actual	Imperial units
Mug	Capacity	260ml	215ml	
TV	Length	82cm	93cm	
Banana	Weight	90g	130g	

Now try to calculate the imperial units for each object.

⚠ Problems

Brain-teaser

Solve these measures problems.

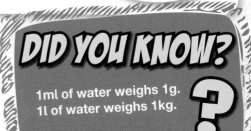

DID YOU KNOW?
1ml of water weighs 1g.
1l of water weighs 1kg.

If it takes 25 seconds to fill a 1 litre jug from a tap, how long will it take to fill three 250ml cups from the same tap? (You can assume that there is no time lost when changing cups.) _____

The 1 litre jug weighs 1.79kg when full of water. What is the weight of the empty jug? _____

The 250ml cup weighs 483g when full of water. What is the weight of the empty cup? _____

Brain-buster

Brian's grandad says that when he was at school he was 4 feet 11 inches tall, and weighed 6 stone, 3 pounds. Convert his height and weight to metric units.

Height _____   Weight _____

If Brian's grandad is 80 on his next birthday, calculate how many days he has lived. (There will have been 20 leap years in his life so far.) _____

How many hours has he lived? _____

How many minutes is this? _____

Perimeter and area

↻ Recap

Perimeter is the distance around the outside of a shape.
All rectangles have a width and a height.
Perimeter can be calculated with a formula:
$P = 2l + 2w$
Or we can say **$P = 2(l + w)$**.

Area is measured in square units. For rectangles
we multiply the length by the width: **$A = lw$**
For this rectangle, $P = 2(3 + 2) = 10$cm, and $A = 3 \times 2 = 6$cm.

The perimeter of a square is four times the length of a side: **$P = 4s$**.
The area of a square is side length times side length: **$A = s^2$**.
The perimeter of this square is: $P = 4 \times 1.5 = 6$cm
The area of this square is: $A = 1.5 \times 1.5 = 2.25$cm²

3cm

2cm

←1.5cm→

📋 Revise

Shapes that have the same perimeter do not necessarily have
the same area as each other.

Shape 1

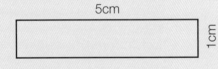

5cm

1cm

Perimeter = 2(5 + 1) = 12cm

Area = 5 × 1 = 5cm²

Shape 2

4cm

2cm

Perimeter = 2(4 + 2) = 12cm

Area = 4 × 2 = 8cm²

> Remember to
> do any calculations in
> brackets first.

💡 Tips

> Here's how to
> get your perimeters
> and areas right.

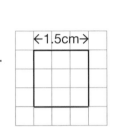

- Watch out for silly mistakes when you find the perimeters and
  areas of composite shapes.
  This shape has a square with a hole in it, joined to a rectangle.
  There are two mistakes that people often make.

  1. They include the perimeter where the shapes are joined. *Don't!*

  2. They forget to take away the area of the hole. *Do!*

💬 Talk maths

You will need a tape measure.
Investigate the perimeter and area of different rectangles and squares around your home.
Measure their lengths and widths, then use formulae to calculate their areas and perimeters.

Object	Shape	Dimensions	Perimeter	Area
Table	Square	$s = 80cm$	320cm	6400cm²
Television	Rectangle	$l = 125cm, w = 75cm$	400cm	9375cm²
Door				

Explain to an adult anything you discover.

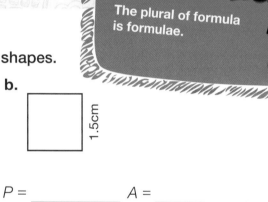

DID YOU KNOW?
The plural of formula is formulae.

✔ Check

1. Calculate the perimeter and area of these shapes.

a.

4.5cm

2cm

$P = $ _____ $A = $ _____

b.

1.5cm

$P = $ _____ $A = $ _____

2. Calculate the perimeter and area of these composite shapes.

a.

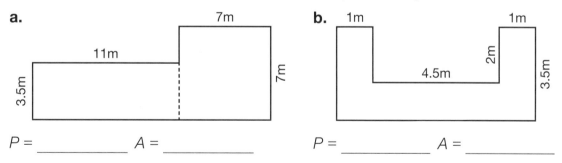

7m

11m

3.5m

7m

$P = $ _____ $A = $ _____

b.

1m   1m

4.5m

2m

3.5m

$P = $ _____ $A = $ _____

⚠ Problems

Brain-teaser Ben's rectangular garden is 5m long and has a total perimeter of 16m.

What is its area? _____

Brain-buster Some square wall tiles are 20cm wide.

How many tiles would be needed to cover a wall 3m high and 2.4m long? _____

Calculating area

↺ Recap

Area is measured in **square units**.
We can count squares for simple areas.
This rectangle has an area of 6cm².
We can use formulae for many shapes.
Formulae help us to find the areas of larger or more complex shapes.
For rectangles we multiply the length by the width: $A = lw$
The formula for the area of a square is $A = s^2$

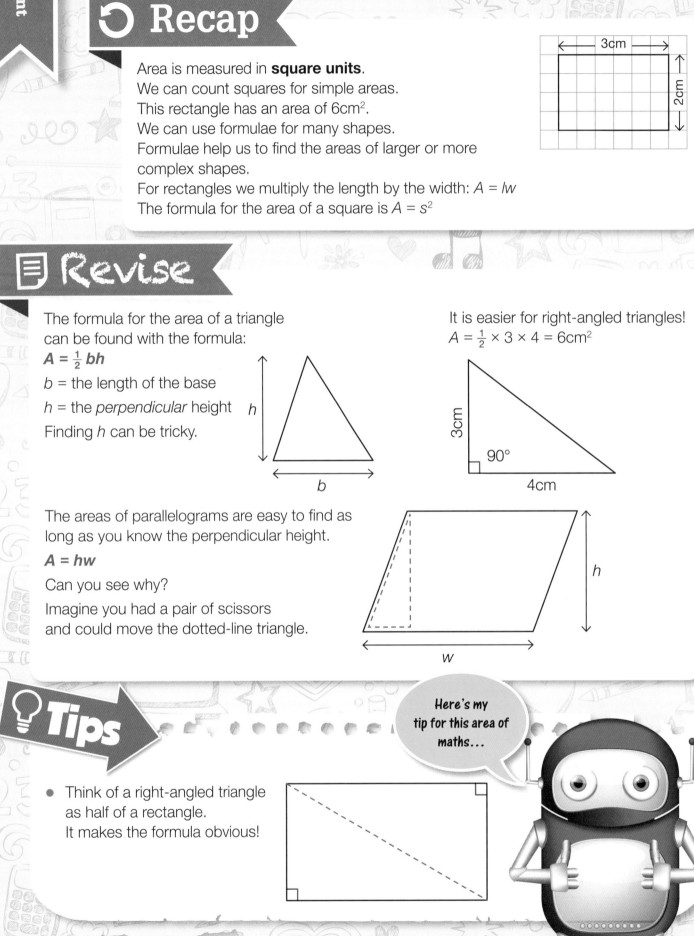

Revise

The formula for the area of a triangle can be found with the formula:

$A = \frac{1}{2} bh$

b = the length of the base

h = the *perpendicular* height

Finding h can be tricky.

It is easier for right-angled triangles!
$A = \frac{1}{2} \times 3 \times 4 = 6cm^2$

The areas of parallelograms are easy to find as long as you know the perpendicular height.

$A = hw$

Can you see why?

Imagine you had a pair of scissors and could move the dotted-line triangle.

💡 Tips

Here's my tip for this area of maths...

- Think of a right-angled triangle as half of a rectangle.
  It makes the formula obvious!

Talk maths

A rectangle is 5m long and 3.5m wide, what is its area?

The sides of a square are 2.5m. What is its area?

Use this chart to challenge a partner to mentally calculate areas. Make up your own side lengths and heights. Be sure to ask questions using the correct vocabulary.

A parallelogram is 4.2m wide and is 3m high. What is its area?

	Rectangle	Square	Triangle	Parallelogram
Shape				
Formula	$A = lw$	$A = s^2$	$A = \frac{1}{2}bh$	$A = wh$

A triangle has a 3cm base and 5cm perpendicular height. What is its area?

✔ Check

1. Calculate the areas of these shapes.

a. 5cm, 4cm

b. 7cm, 5cm

c. 4.5cm, 5cm

2. Underline which shape has the larger area.

a. A rectangle, length 7cm and width 4cm　OR　a square with sides 5.5cm

b. A parallelogram, length 9m and height 3m　OR　a triangle, base 12m and height 5m

c. A triangle, base 5cm and height 7cm　OR　a rectangle, base 6cm and height 2.5cm

⚠ Problems

Brain-teaser A carpet costs £23 per square metre.

How much would it cost to carpet a room that is 5.3m long and 4.2m wide? _____

Brain-buster In this shape, the height and base of the triangular hole are exactly half the length of the sides of the square.

What is the shaded area? _____

3 m

Calculating volume

Sometimes faces are called sides.

↻ Recap

3D shapes have faces, edges and vertices.

A corner is a **vertex**. The plural is **vertices**.

Volume is the amount of space an object takes up. Volume isn't quite the same as capacity. We measure capacity in litres, centilitres or millilitres; we measure volume in cubic lengths: km³, m³, cm³, mm³.

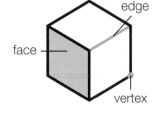

📝 Revise

A cubic centimetre is a cube that has length, width and height all equal to 1cm.

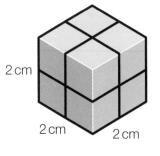

A cube that has sides of length 2cm has a volume of 8cm³. A *cube* is a 3D shape that has all sides the same length.

You need to be careful with units.
1cm³ = 10mm × 10mm × 10mm = 1000mm³
1m³ = 100cm × 100cm × 100cm = 1,000,000cm³

We can use formulae for calculating the volumes of cubes and cuboids.

Volume of cube = s^3 (s = length of one side)
A cubes of with side 3cm has a volume of
3cm × 3cm × 3cm = 27cm³

Volume of cuboid = whl (w = width, h = height, l = length)
A cuboid with width 4cm, height 2cm and length 5cm has a volume of 4cm × 2cm × 5cm = 40cm³.

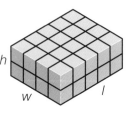

A *cuboid* has rectangular faces, but they are not all the same size.

💡 Tips

Here's my advice for perfecting your 3D drawings...

- Drawing shapes to look 3D is called *isometric drawing*. The trick is to draw one end face, and then draw the edges as parallel lines.

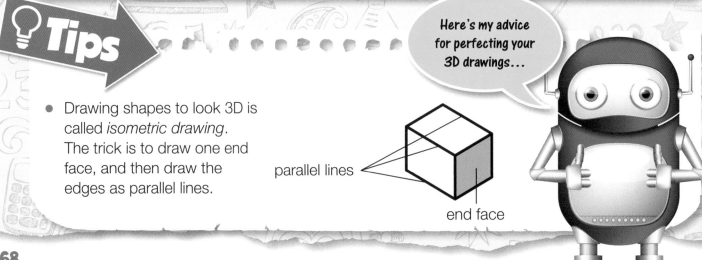

parallel lines

end face

Talk maths

Work with an adult or a friend to discuss how you might estimate the volume of large objects. For example in a bathroom you could estimate that the room is 3m high, 4m long and 2m wide. So the volume of the bathroom could be estimated as 24m³.

What about the volume of a bath?

Or even the volume of your house?

✔ Check

1. Use a pencil and ruler to draw each of these shapes.

    a. A cube with side length 3cm

    b. A cuboid, length 5cm, height 2cm, width 4cm

2. Calculate the volume of these shapes.

    a. Cube, side 6cm _____

    b. Cuboid, *l* = 6m, *w* = 4m, *h* = 1.5m _____

    c. Cube, side 10m _____

    d. Cuboid, *l* = 9cm, *w* = 5cm, *h* = 2cm _____

    e. Cube, side 12mm _____

    f. Cuboid, *l* = 60mm, *w* = 30mm, *h* = 5mm _____

3. How many cubic millimetres are there in 1m³? _____

⚠ Problems

Brain-teaser A cube-shaped packing crate is 0.5m long on each side.

Calculate its volume: in m³ _____ in cm³ _____

Brain-buster A wooden cuboid has a square-shaped hole cut right through its middle.

What is the volume of the remaining wood? _____

3.5m

1.5m

0.5m

0.5m

8.4m

Angles

We measure angles with a protractor.

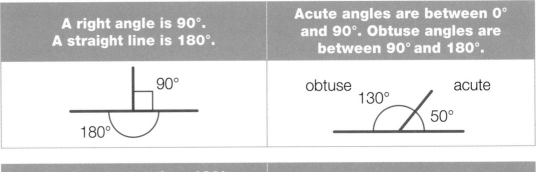

A right angle is 90°. A straight line is 180°.	Acute angles are between 0° and 90°. Obtuse angles are between 90° and 180°.
90° 180°	obtuse acute 130° 50°

Angles greater than 180° are called *reflex* angles.	A complete turn is 360°.
200° reflex	360°

📝 Revise

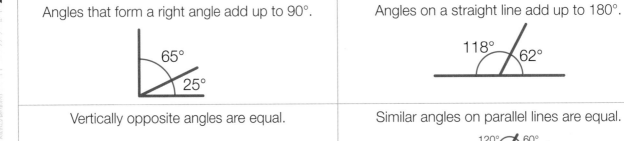

Angles that form a right angle add up to 90°.	Angles on a straight line add up to 180°.
65° 25°	118° 62°
Vertically opposite angles are equal.	Similar angles on parallel lines are equal.
30° 30°	120° 60° 60° 120° 120° 60° 60° 120°

💡 Tips

- Once you understand how angles work, identifying and constructing shapes is easy!
  - The three angles of a triangle add up to 180°.
  - Each angle of an equilvalent triangle = 60°.
  - The four angles of a quadrilateral add up to 360°.
  - Each angle of square and rectangle = 90°

> When drawing shapes, let's talk angles.

Talk maths

Try out your presentation on an adult!

You will need a paper, a pencil, a ruler and a protractor.

Prepare a presentation that will explain different types of angles from page 68.

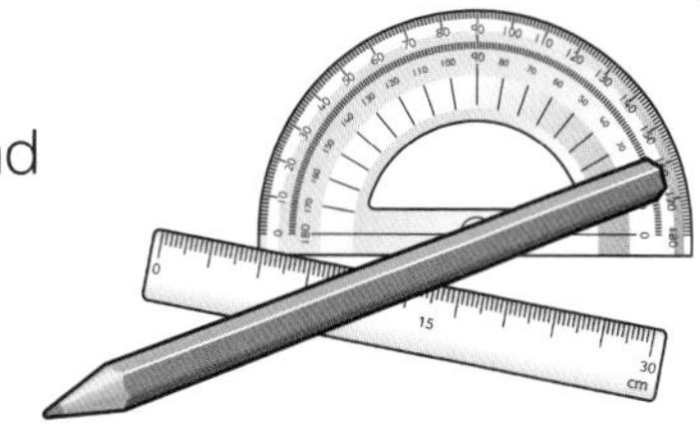

✔ Check

1. **Use a protractor to draw these angles, and then name them.**

   a. 90°

   b. 23°

   c. 167°

   Name: _____

   Name: _____

   Name: _____

2. **Write down the value of each angle marked with a letter.**

   a.

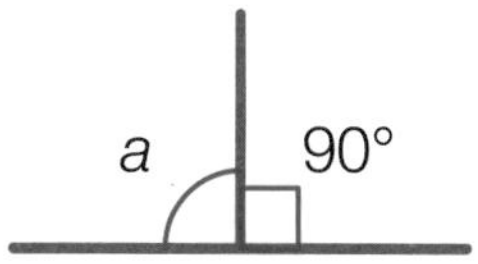

   a   90°

   b.

   b   37°

   c.

   c

   65°

   angle *a* = _____

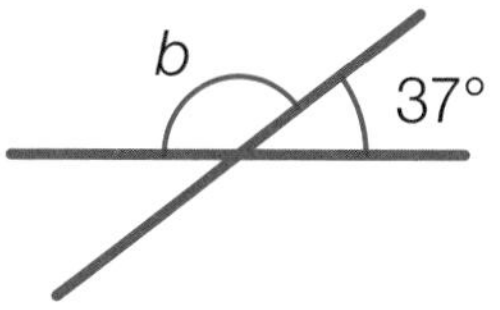

   angle *b* = _____

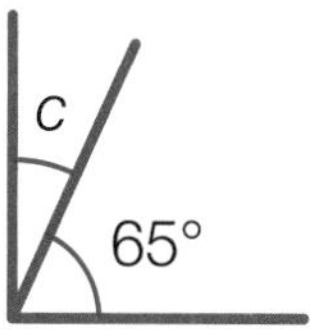

   angle *c* = _____

⚠ Problems

Brain-teaser Two parallel lines are intersected by another line. There are eight different angles.
Without using a protractor, complete the size of every angle in the diagram.

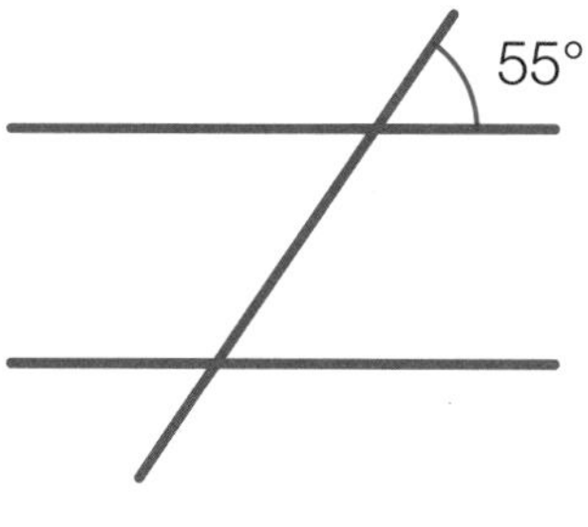

55°

Brain-buster This shape is a parallelogram – its opposite sides are parallel. How can you use it to prove that the four angles of a quadrilateral add up to 360°?

_____

_____

Properties of 2D shapes

↻ Recap

There are different types of triangles. Each has different properties.

Equilateral	Isosceles	Right-angled	Scalene
▲	▲	◢	◢
All sides equal All angles 60°	Two sides equal Two angles equal	One angle equals 90°	All sides different All angles different

Quadrilaterals also have different properties.

Square	Rectangle	Rhombus	Parallelogram	Kite	Trapezium
■	▬	▱	▰	◆	⬯
All sides equal All angles 90°	Opposite sides equal All angles 90°	All sides equal Opposite angles equal	Opposite sides equal and parallel Opposite angles equal	Adjacent sides equal	Only one pair of parallel sides

📋 Revise

> Internal angles is a posh name for angles at the corners.

We say that different 2D polygons have different properties.
The sum of internal angles is the same for each shape, whether irregular or regular.

Triangle	Quadrilateral	Pentagon	Hexagon	Heptagon	Octagon
3 sides	4 sides	5 sides	6 sides	7 sides	8 sides
Angles add to 180°	Angles add to 360°	Angles add to 540°	Angles add to 720°	Angles add to 900°	Angles add to 1080°

💡 Tips

> Think triangles!

- Take any regular shape and divide it into equal triangles.

  The total of the angles at the centre must be 360°, so we can work out each angle around the centre by dividing 360° by the number of triangles. The angles of a triangle all add to 180°, so we can work out the other angles of the triangle, and then the angles at each corner of the shape.

  Look at this regular pentagon. Can you see why each internal angle is 108°?

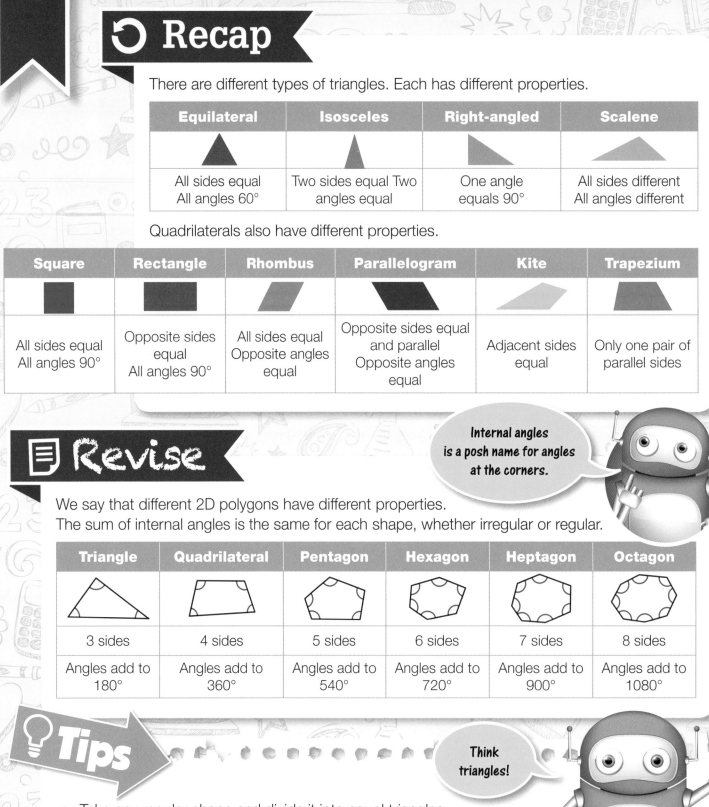

Talk maths

You will need a protractor, a ruler, a pencil and paper.
Work with a friend or an adult to investigate the angles
inside the six regular shapes.
Read though the information and tips on the previous page,
and discuss how you will approach your investigation.

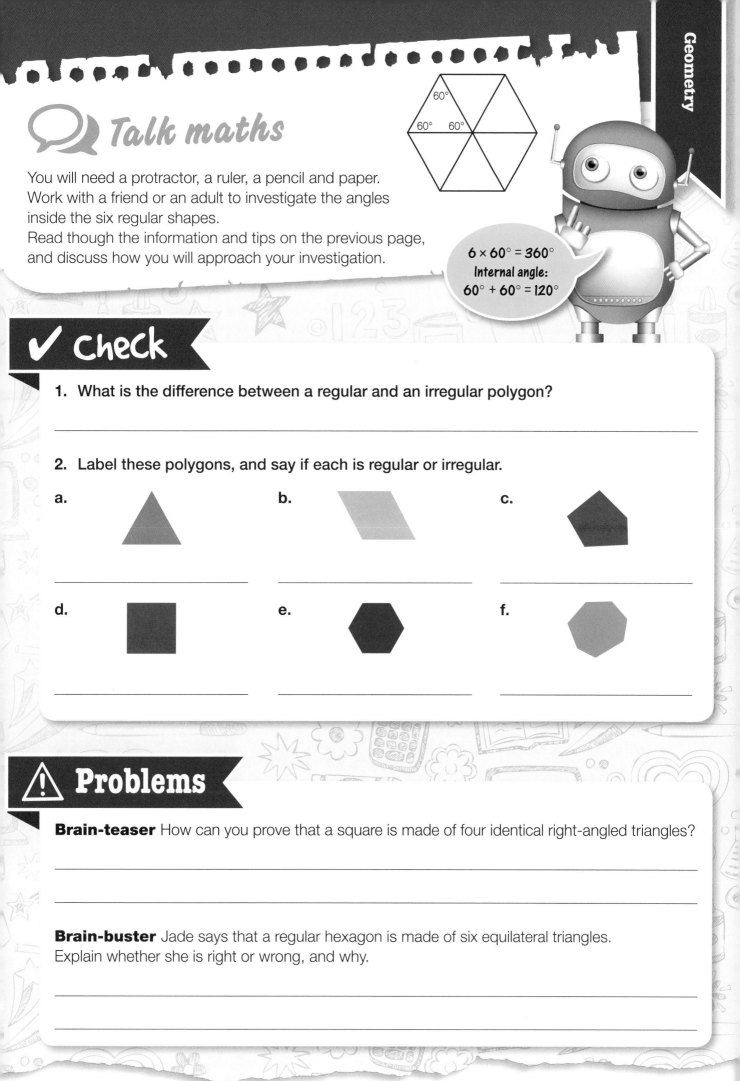

6 × 60° = 360°
Internal angle:
60° + 60° = 120°

✔ Check

1. What is the difference between a regular and an irregular polygon?

_____

2. Label these polygons, and say if each is regular or irregular.

a.

_____

b.

_____

c.

_____

d.

_____

e.

_____

f.

_____

⚠ Problems

Brain-teaser How can you prove that a square is made of four identical right-angled triangles?

_____

_____

Brain-buster Jade says that a regular hexagon is made of six equilateral triangles.
Explain whether she is right or wrong, and why.

_____

_____

Drawing 2D shapes

↻ Recap

A polygon is any straight-sided 2D shape. These are regular polygons. For each shape the internal angles are the same size and the sides are the same length.

Triangle	Quadrilateral	Pentagon	Hexagon	Heptagon	Octagon
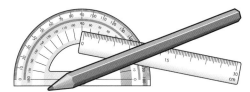					
3 sides	4 sides	5 sides	6 sides	7 sides	8 sides
Angles add to 180°	Angles add to 360°	Angles add to 540°	Angles add to 720°	Angles add to 900°	Angles add to 1080°

📋 Revise

To draw any triangle you need to know two angle sizes and one side length. Or two side lengths and one angle.

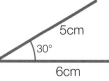

To draw a square, rectangle, rhombus or parallelogram you only need to know one angle size and two side lengths.

parallelogram 4cm 1cm 100°

rhombus 2cm 2cm 120°

rectangle 3cm 2cm 90°

square 3cm 3cm 90°

There is a link between geometry and algebra, because we can write formulae for different shapes. If the angles of a triangle are a, b and c, we can say $a + b + c = 180°$.

> **Can you think of formulae for the angles in other regular polygons?**

💡 Tips

- You need to know how to draw 2D shapes. Remember that all regular pentagons (five sides), hexagons (six sides), heptagons (seven sides) and octagons (eight sides) are all made of identical triangles.
- Also remember that all the angles at the centre add up to 360°.

💬 Talk maths

Draw a rhombus with sides of 5cm and two angles of 125°.

Play this game with a partner. You will need pencils, paper, a ruler and a protractor. Take turns to challenge each other to construct shapes, giving verbal instructions. Remember to give enough information, for example: *Draw an isosceles triangle with a base of 6cm and two angles of 65°.*

Draw a regular hexagon with sides of 4cm.

✔ Check

1. Draw an equilateral triangle with each side 4cm.

2. Draw a rhombus, with sides 3cm and the larger angle = 120°.

3. Explain how you would construct a regular octagon.

_____

_____

⚠ Problems

Brain-teaser The five internal angles of a regular pentagon add up to 540°. A ten-sided shape is called a decagon. What will the internal angles of a regular decagon add up to? Show your working out.

_____

_____

Brain-buster Can you write a formula for calculating the size of each angle in a regular polygon, where a = the angle and n = the number of sides? _____

3D shapes

↻ Recap

3D shapes have different properties which identify them.

Shape							
Name	Cube	Cuboid	Cone	Sphere	Cylinder	Triangular prism	Square-based pyramid
Faces	6	6	2	1	3	5	5
Edges	12	12	1	0	2	9	8
Vertices	8	8	0	0	0	6	5

📝 Revise

Some 3D shapes can be represented by **nets**. A net is a 2D drawing of the shape as if it has been taken apart, or unfolded. The skill is in thinking about which edges meet.

There is more than one way to make a net, and plenty of ways to get it wrong! Look at these cube nets.

You cannot make accurate nets for spheres or cones because they have curved faces. Try peeling an orange and laying it flat – it cannot be done accurately.

That is why maps of the world are tricky to make.

That is why maps of the world are tricky to make.

Mark it. Tab it. Net it!

💡 Tips

- When looking at, or drawing, nets, use marks to help you see if the sides match up correctly. Use tabs to help you to join the faces together.

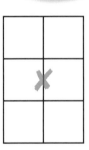

💬 Talk maths

You will need squared paper, a ruler and a pencil.
Work with a partner to construct three cuboids of different sizes, making nets for each one. When you have finished, discuss the steps you took to make a successful net, then explain these instructions to someone else and see if they can make a net using your advice.

> Remember, you only need one tab to join two faces.

✔ Check

1. **Add tabs to these nets so that the faces would join together.**

   a. Pyramid

   b. Prism

   c. Cuboid

2. **Draw a net for a cube with 2cm edges. Include tabs to join the faces together.**

⚠ Problems

Brain-teaser Write instructions for how to make a paper model of a square-based pyramid.

_____

_____

_____

Brain-buster Ryan has a sheet of paper 30cm long and 20cm wide.

a. What is the largest cuboid he can make from it? _____

b. How much paper will be wasted (in cm²)? _____

c. What will be the volume of the cuboid? _____

Circles

↺ Recap

A circle is a single line that is always the same distance from its centre.

We can draw circles using a pair of compasses.

📄 Revise

The edge of a circle is called the **circumference**.

The distance across the centre of a circle is called the **diameter**.

The distance from the circumference to the centre is called the **radius**.

The diameter is twice the length of the radius.

We write this using the formula: **d = 2r**

You can estimate the circumference of a circle using thread or string, and you can estimate area by counting squares and parts of squares.

diameter
radius
circumference

> Remember, circles are 2D shapes, and spheres are 3D.

💡 Tips

- You can draw a circle using only string and a pencil. Tie the pencil to the string and hold the string tightly where you want the centre of the circle to be.

  Try drawing different-sized circles just using string.

💬 Talk maths

> The string might help you measure the circumference.

You will need some string, a ruler, a compass and a pencil.

Working with a partner, find a selection of approximately ten circular objects. Using your equipment, find the radius, diameter and circumference for each one. Make sure you agree on each measurement before you add it to a table.

Discuss the connection between the size of the circumference and the size of the diameter or the radius?

Object	Radius	Diameter	Circumference
10p	1.25cm	2.5cm	7.85cm
DVD	6cm	12cm	37.5cm
Bike wheel	25cm	50cm	157cm

✔ Check

1. Explain these terms.

   a. radius: _____

   b. diameter: _____

   c. circumference: _____

2. If a circle has a radius of 3.5m, what is its diameter? _____

3. A circular field has a diameter of 1.5km. What is its radius? _____

⚠ Problems

Brain-teaser Aaron says that the circumference of any circle is just over five times its diameter. Looking at this circle, would you say he is right? Explain your answer.

_____

_____

Brain-buster Meena says that the area of any circle is approximately three times the radius squared, or $3r^2$. Looking at this circle, would you say she is right? Explain your answer, using calculations if necessary.

_____

_____

Positive and negative coordinates

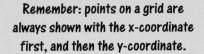

Remember: points on a grid are always shown with the x-coordinate first, and then the y-coordinate.

↺ Recap

We can plot points anywhere on a coordinate grid to make lines or to show the vertices of shapes.

The co-ordinates of B are (2,6).

The triangle's vertices coordinates are (3, 1), (5, 1) and (4, 3).

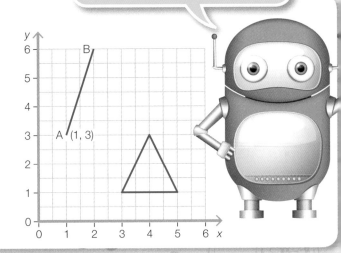

📋 Revise

Grids can have negative axes too. They are just like number lines.

We say the coordinate grid has four **quadrants**.

Coordinates are positive and negative according to which quadrant they are in.

Remember, the point where the axes meet is called the origin. The coordinates of the origin are (0, 0).

Look at the points on the coordinate grids. Each one has its coordinates next to it.
The coordinates of A are (3, 6).

The axes are like thermometers!

💡 Tips

- Each quadrant will always be positive or negative for *x* and *y*.
  1st quadrant: *x* and *y* positive
  2nd quadrant: *x* negative, *y* positive
  3rd quadrant: *x* and *y* negative
  4th quadrant: *x* positive, *y* negative
- Remember, for reading coordinates it's along first, then up.

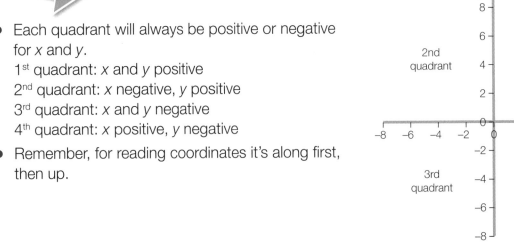

Talk maths

Where is the point (−5, −8)?

Draw a coordinate grid with four quadrants, with each axes going from −8 to +8, or use one of the grids on these pages. Working with a partner, challenge each other to identify points in particular quadrants.

Show me a point in the second quadrant. What are its coordinates?

✔ Check

1. a. Write the coordinates of each point marked on the coordinate grid.

A: (_____ , _____) B: (_____ , _____)
C: (_____ , _____)   D: (_____ , _____)

b. What shape do they make?

_____

c. Write the coordinates of the centre of the shape.

_____

2. a. Mark these points on the grid.

P (3, 5) Q (−1, 5) R (−4, −1) S (0, −1)

b. What shape do they make? _____

⚠ Problems

Brain-teaser What shape do these points make when joined together?

A (0, 6), B (−3, 4), C (0, −2), D (3, 4) _____

Brain-buster A rectangle's centre is at the point (2, 1) and the coordinates of one vertex is at (7, 6).
Write the coordinates of the other three vertices and say which quadrant each is in.

	Quadrant	Coordinates
Vertex 1	1	(7, 6)
Vertex 2		
Vertex 3		
Vertex 4		

Reflecting and translating shapes

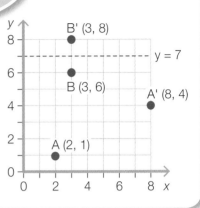

Why did only the y-coordinate change?

↻ Recap

When we translate points, we say how much the x and y coordinates change.
For example, A (2, 1) to A¹ (8, 4)
x has increased by +6
and y has increased by +3.

When we reflect points, the line of reflection acts like a mirror, and the coordinates of the reflected points change. For example, B (3, 6) to B¹ (3, 8)

Revise

For four-quadrant grids, we can translate and reflect in the same way.

Rectangle PQRS has been **translated**. Each vertex of the rectangle moves by the same amount. Can you see what the missing numbers are?

For P¹Q¹R¹S¹, $x = +9$ $y = -10$

We can also reflect points and shapes in the x-axis and y-axis.
Notice how the triangle ABC has changed; it has been **reflected** in the x-axis.
WXYZ has been **reflected** in the y-axis. What has happened to each vertex of the square?

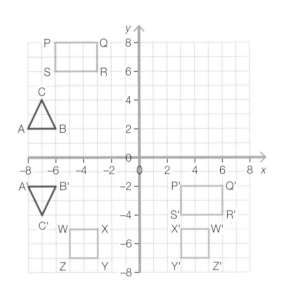

Tips

- **Reflections**
  For reflections in the y-axis, only the x-coordinates change: they reverse their sign.
  For reflections in the x-axis, only the y-coordinates change: they reverse their sign.

- **Translations**
  We can write translations as, for example, $x - 8, y + 6$, or whatever the translation is.
  Remember, for shapes, every vertex will be translated by the same amount.

Talk maths

You will need a pencil, a ruler and a rubber. Carefully draw a shape on this grid and challenge someone to reflect or translate it by giving them precise instructions.

Ask them to give you the new coordinates of the shape.

Draw your shapes gently and then rub them out so that you can repeat the challenge a few times. As an extra tricky challenge, reflect a shape and then translate it too.

Reflect the square in the y-axis.

Translate the triangle by x + 3, y − 2.

✔ Check

1. Using the coordinate grid opposite.

   a. Translate the shape PQRS by x − 3 and y + 2.

   b. Reflect the shape WXYZ in the y-axis.

   c. Reflect the shape WXYZ in the x-axis.

2. A triangle A (6, 2) B (0, 5) C (−1, −3) is reflected in the x-axis to create triangle A^{1}B^{1}C^1. Write the coordinates of each new vertex.

   A^1 (_____, _____)   B^1 (_____, _____)   C^1 (_____, _____)

3. The triangle D (0, 0) E (3, −3) F (−1, −2) is translated by x − 2, y − 4 to create triangle D^{1}E^{1}F^1. Write the coordinates of each new vertex.

   D^1 (_____, _____)   E^1 (_____, _____)   F^1 (_____, _____)

⚠ Problems

Brain-teaser What is unusual about reflecting the square P (3, −2) Q (3, −8) R (−3, −8) S (−3, −2) in the y-axis?

_____

Brain-buster Sam says that reflecting the square ABCD in the x-axis and then in the y-axis is the same as translating it x + 9, y + 7. Is he right?

Explain your answer. _____

_____

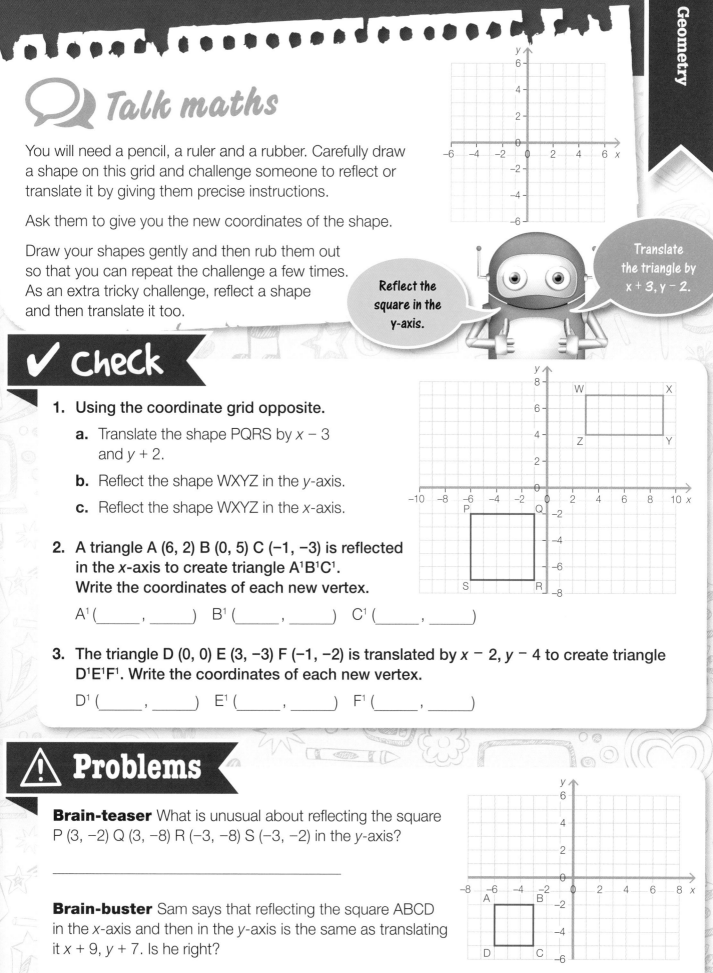

Pie charts

> Different graphs are used for different situations and different types of data.

↺ Recap

We can represent information and data in different types of charts and graphs.

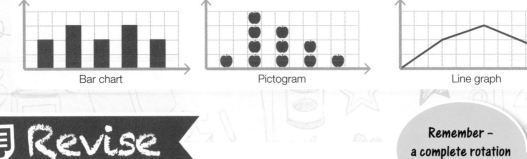

Bar chart   Pictogram   Line graph   Pie chart

📝 Revise

> Remember – a complete rotation has 360°.

Pie charts use fractions of circles to represent quantities.
They are great for helping us to see proportions at a glance.

This pie chart shows the different proportion of journeys to school made by all children in Britain.

Because a complete rotation is 360°, any fraction or percentage is shown as an angle, as a part of 360°.

Look at the same information in a chart.

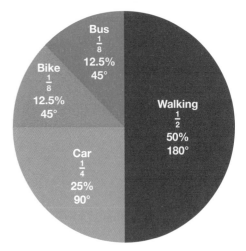

Transport	Walking	Car	Bike	Bus
Fraction	$\frac{1}{2}$	$\frac{1}{4}$	$\frac{1}{8}$	$\frac{1}{8}$
Percentage	50%	25%	12.5%	12.5%
Angle on pie chart	180°	90°	45°	45°

Although this pie chart doesn't show us the actual number of journeys, we can still work these out. If the total number of journeys to school each day in Britain was 10 million, we can use the pie chart to calculate numbers for each of the journey types. For example, 5 million children must walk, because 5 million is half of 10 million.

💡 Tips

- To understand pie charts you need to convert angles, fractions and percentages. Try to learn the main ones.

Angle	3.6°	18°	36°	45°	90°	180°	360°
Fraction	$\frac{1}{100}$	$\frac{1}{20}$	$\frac{1}{10}$	$\frac{1}{8}$	$\frac{1}{4}$	$\frac{1}{2}$	$\frac{1}{1}$
Percentage	1%	5%	10%	12.5%	25%	50%	100%

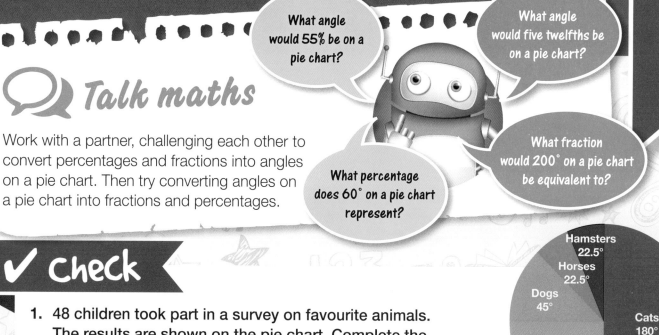

Talk maths

Work with a partner, challenging each other to convert percentages and fractions into angles on a pie chart. Then try converting angles on a pie chart into fractions and percentages.

What angle would 55% be on a pie chart?

What angle would five twelfths be on a pie chart?

What fraction would 200° on a pie chart be equivalent to?

What percentage does 60° on a pie chart represent?

✔ Check

1. 48 children took part in a survey on favourite animals. The results are shown on the pie chart. Complete the table to show how many children prefer each type of animal.

Animal	Cats	Guinea pigs	Dogs	Horses	Hamsters
Angle	180°	90°	45°	22.5°	22.5°
Children					

Hamsters 22.5°
Horses 22.5°
Dogs 45°
Guinea pigs 90°
Cats 180°

2. You will need a protractor to do this activity.
A family of five are on holiday. They need to catch a taxi and they only have loose change in their pockets. Draw a pie chart to show the proportion each person contributes to the total amount.

Mum	Dad	Paul	Lizzie	Mary
£1.80	5p	45p	£1.20	10p

⚠ Problems

The pie chart shows the population of the world by continent.

Brain-teaser Without measuring, can you estimate the angle for Europe in the pie chart?

_____

Brain-buster If the population of the world is 7 billion, estimate the population of each continent, to the nearest tenth of a billion.

■ Asia
■ Europe
■ North America
■ South America
■ Oceania
■ Africa

Asia	Africa	Europe	Oceania	North America	South America
4.2 billion					

Your estimates should add up to around 7 billion!

Line graphs

↻ Recap

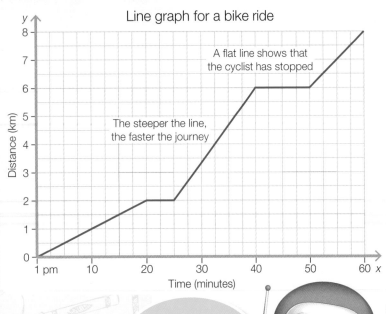

Line graph for a bike ride

A flat line shows that the cyclist has stopped

The steeper the line, the faster the journey

Distance (km) / Time (minutes)

Line graphs are useful for showing how things change over time, such as temperature, growth and speed. Normally time is shown along the horizontal x-axis.

Remember, to read a graph, you go along the x-axis and up the y-axis.

This graph shows the time taken for an 8km cycle ride.

Find these bits of information on the graph.

- The journey starts at 1pm.
- After 20 minutes the cyclist stops for five minutes.
- The cyclist travels fastest from 25 minutes to 40 minutes.
- The cyclist stops again after 40 minutes.
- The journey finishes at 8km.

Look carefully at the scale on each axis.

📄 Revise

Line graphs can also be used for converting similar quantities that have different units, such as temperatures, distances and currencies.

This graph can be used for converting US dollars to pounds.

The direction of the line is affected by how many dollars there are for every pound. In this graph

£1 = \$1.5   £5 = \$7.5   \$9 = £6

How many dollars would you get for £5?

How many pounds would you get for \$9?

💡 Tips

- Use a pencil and a ruler for accurate conversions. Remember that you need to read graphs carefully – use a ruler to help you read horizontal and vertical coordinates.

💬 Talk maths

How many kilometres in 50 miles?

Practise converting miles to kilometres, and kilometres to miles, using this line graph.

How many kilometres are there in 2 miles? How many miles are there in 5 kilometres? Can you use the graph to work out larger distances?

(Graph with y-axis labelled "Miles" from 0 to 10, x-axis labelled "Kilometres" from 0 to 20, showing a straight diagonal line from origin.)

✔ Check

1. **The line graph shows the distance travelled on a charity walk.**

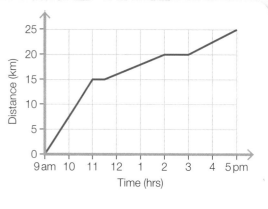

a. Why is the line horizontal from 11am to 11.30am, and from 2pm to 3pm?

_____

_____

b. How far did the walkers travel from 3pm to 5pm? _____

c. The fastest part of the journey was from 9am to 11am. At what speed were the walkers travelling then? _____

d. Another group of walkers started walking at 12 noon and walked at a constant speed and arrived at the end exactly the same time as the other group. Draw their journey on the graph with a dotted line.

e. What was the speed of the second set of walkers? _____

⚠ Problems

This is the formula for converting temperatures from Fahrenheit to Celsius: $C = \frac{5}{9} \times (F - 32)$
It can be used to create a line graph.
Draw the line graph on square paper and then use it to solve these problems.

Brain-teaser Water boils at 100°C. What is that in degrees Fahrenheit? _____

Brain-buster Where does the line cross the *y*-axis? _____

Where does the line cross the *x*-axis? _____

Averages

We can collect data and represent it in tables, charts and graphs.

For example, this bar chart shows the number of vegetarian school lunches eaten each day for a week.
We call this collection of information a data set.

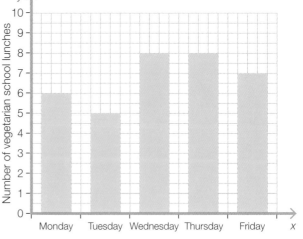

Revise

A mean is the average of the data set.
To find the mean, add together all of the numbers and then divide it by how many numbers there are.

Day	Monday	Tuesday	Wednesday	Thursday	Friday
Vegetarian lunches	6	5	8	8	7

Using the above definitions, we can find out the mean for this data set.
Mean = (6 + 5 + 8 + 8 + 7) ÷ 5
= 34 ÷ 5 = 6.8

We can say, on average, 6.8 vegetarian lunches are eaten each day.

Tips

- Remember, the mean average is not always a whole number.

  Mean averages are useful for comparing things. For example, the number of people going on holiday in the summer, is higher than at other times. The mean average for holidays in a year would be very different to just the summer months.

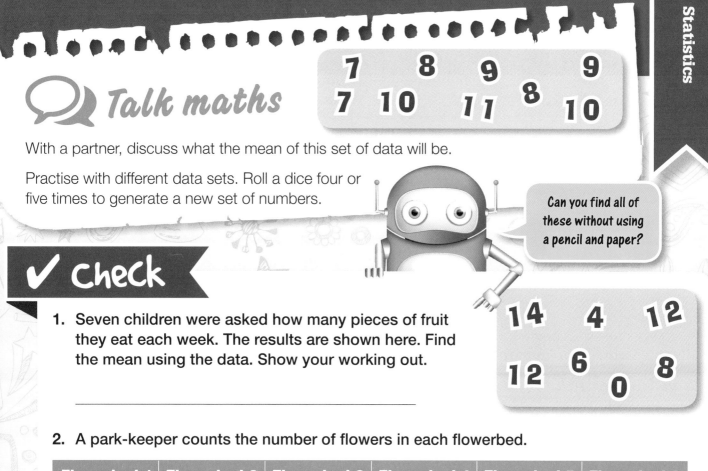

Talk maths

| 7 | 8 | 9 | 9 |
| 7 | 10 | 11 | 8 | 10 |

With a partner, discuss what the mean of this set of data will be.

Practise with different data sets. Roll a dice four or five times to generate a new set of numbers.

Can you find all of these without using a pencil and paper?

✔ Check

1. Seven children were asked how many pieces of fruit they eat each week. The results are shown here. Find the mean using the data. Show your working out.

| 14 | 4 | 12 |
| 12 | 6 | 0 | 8 |

_____

2. A park-keeper counts the number of flowers in each flowerbed.

Flowerbed 1	Flowerbed 2	Flowerbed 3	Flowerbed 4	Flowerbed 5	Flowerbed 6
23	25	20	23	26	28

   a. Find the total number of flowers in the park. _____

   b. Find the mean number of flowers per flowerbed. _____

⚠ Problems

Brain-teaser Just before the summer holidays, ten Year 6 children each estimate (to the nearest five) how many books they have read in their time in the Juniors. Calculate the mean.

Aaron	Fahad	Beth	Jin	Eva	Scarlett	Mason	Sam	Jayden	Zac
45	50	75	35	50	90	40	50	45	80

_____

Brain-buster Gemma is reading a novel and wants to estimate how many words she has read. She counts the words on six different pages: 274   286   259   262   294   272

What is the average number of words per page? _____

If the book is 386 pages long, and 20 of the pages are only half full (because they start or end a chapter), estimate how many words in total are in the book. _____

Answers: Year 6

NUMBER AND PLACE VALUE

Page 9

1. **a.** 350 **b.** 190 **c.** 3500 **d.** 1666

2. **a.** four hundred or 400 **b.** thirty thousand or 30,000
    c. four million or 4,000,000 **d.** six hundred thousand or
    600,000

Brain-teaser 1,000,001
Brain-buster 9,999,999
Nine million, nine hundred and ninety-nine thousand, nine hundred
and ninety-nine

Page 11

1 Eight hundred and forty-five thousand, two hundred and
   eighty-three

2 604,190

3 Six hundred thousand or 600,000

4 97,612 500,000 825,421 6,899,372 10,000,000

5 **a.** 3521 < 5630 **b.** 15,204 > 9798
   c. 833,521 > 795,732

Brain-teaser Madrid
Brain-buster Paris, Rome, Madrid

Page 13

1 **a.** 5000 **b.** 23,000 **c.** 45,000 **d.** 79,000

2 **a.** 100,000 **b.** 500,000 **c.** 1,400,000 **d.** 8,000,000

3 **a.** 6,000,000 **b.** 1,000,000 **c.** 4,000,000 **d.** 10,000,000

4 **a.** 0, 100,000, 200,000, 300,000, 400,000, 500,000
   b. 370,000, 380,000, 390,000, 400,000, 410,000
   c. 7,500,000, 8,500,000, 9,500,000, 10,500,000, 11,500,000

Brain-teaser

City	Rome	Paris	Madrid
Population	3,000,000	2,000,000	3,000,000

Brain-buster 8,000,000. This is lower than the actual total
because there has been more rounding down than rounding up.

Page 15

1 **a.** –2 **b.** –4 **c.** 3 **d.** 0

2 –20 –16 –12 –8 –4 0 4 8 12 16 20

3 **a.** – **b.** + **c.** – **d.** –

4 **a.** 14 **b.** 19 **c.** 7 **d.** –9

Brain-teaser 8°C
Brain-buster 69.4°C

CALCULATIONS

Page 17

1 **a.** 792 **b.** 5526 **c.** 479,369

2 **a.** 540 **b.** 117,450 **c.** 2355

3 **a.** 548,704 **b.** 962,825 **c.** 5,167,467

4 **a.** 79,740 **b.** 635,231 **c.** 2,482,597

Brain-teaser 982,136
Brain-buster 8,312,272

Page 19

1 **a.** 4800 **b.** 62,000 **c.** 1600 **d.** 50,000 **e.** 430,000
   f. 1,000,000

2 **a.** 2000 **b.** 25 **c.** 40,000 **d.** 90,000 **e.** 80,001
   f. 25,000

3 **a.** 27,072 **b.** 723

Brain-teaser £160,000
Brain-buster 3000 tickets

Page 21

1. **a.** 868 **b.** 7150 **c.** 13,770 **d.** 329,576

2. **a.** 8925 **b.** 38,010 **c.** 79,890 **d.** 567,840

Brain-teaser 24,984 (!)
Brain-buster £729,723

Page 23

1 **a.** 23 **b.** 24 r3 **c.** 434 r1 **d.** 313 r2

2 **a.** 12 r2 **b.** 64 r2 **c.** 460 r5 **d.** 1132 r4

Brain-teaser 13 each with 2 stickers left over
Brain-buster 1248 tickets
You can check your answer by multiplying the number of tickets by
the ticket price.

Page 25

1 **a.** 210 r14 **b.** 254 r8

2 **a.** 22 r8 **b.** 211 r7 **c.** 353 r4 **d.** 228 r22

Brain-teaser 134 rows
Brain-buster £2341.75

Page 27

1 **a.** 0 **b.** 6 **c.** 27

2 **a.** 2 **b.** 12 **c.** 5

3 **a.** correct **b.** correct **c.** incorrect (–7) **d.** correct

4 **a.** 8 × (5 + 2) – 3 = 53 **b.** 14 ÷ 7 + 2 × (11 – 6) = 12
   c. 64 – (12 + 5 × 3) = 37

Brain-teaser Yes. (34 + 17 + 43) × 2 – 20 = 168
Could also be expressed as (34 x 2) + (17 x 2) + (43 x 2) –20 =
168
Brain-buster 12,000 × 2 + (7000 – 2500) × 3 = £37,500
2 new cars and 3 second hand cars.

Page 29

1 1, 2 and 4

2 1, 2, 5 and 10

3 15, 30, 45, 60, 75, 90, etc.

4 2 × 5 × 7 = 70

5 2, 3 and 5

6 94: 2 × 47

Brain-teaser 38 has prime factors, but it is not a prime number.
Prime numbers only have themselves and 1 as factors.
Brain-buster 6

FRACTIONS, DECIMALS AND PERCENTAGES

Page 31

1 **a.** 2 **b.** 3 **c.** 1 **d.** 20 **e.** 30 **f.** 11

2 **a.** True **b.** True **c.** False **d.** True

3 **a.** $\frac{3}{4}$ **b.** $\frac{3}{4}$ **c.** $\frac{3}{4}$ **d.** $\frac{3}{4}$ **e.** $\frac{9}{20}$ **f.** $\frac{5}{8}$ **g.** $\frac{32}{75}$ **h.** $\frac{8}{25}$

Brain-teaser $\frac{8}{25}$

Brain-buster $\frac{17}{25}$

Page 33

1 **a.** $\frac{15}{30}$ **b.** $\frac{20}{30}$ **c.** $\frac{18}{30}$ **d.** $\frac{25}{30}$

2 **a.** = **b.** > **c.** > **d.** <

3 **a.** True **b.** True **c.** False

4 **a.** $\frac{5}{8} < \frac{2}{3} < \frac{3}{4}$ **b.** $\frac{1}{3} < \frac{3}{7} < \frac{4}{9}$ **c.** $\frac{13}{24} < \frac{5}{9} < \frac{7}{12}$

Brain-teaser $\frac{3}{8}$ ($\frac{3}{8} = \frac{15}{40}$ and $\frac{7}{20} = \frac{14}{40}$)

Brain-buster cats ($\frac{21}{84}$) or $\frac{3}{12}$) < dogs ($\frac{24}{84}$ or $\frac{2}{7}$)) < no pets ($\frac{39}{84}$ or $\frac{13}{28}$)

Page 35

1   **a.** $\frac{5}{6}$ **b.** $\frac{7}{10}$ **c.** $\frac{7}{8}$

2   **a.** $\frac{1}{8}$ **b.** $\frac{4}{9}$ **c.** $\frac{11}{60}$

3   **a.** + **b.** − **c.** + **d.** − **e.** − **f.** +

4   **a.** $4\frac{1}{4}$ **b.** $1\frac{1}{4}$ **c.** $1\frac{2}{15}$ **d.** $4\frac{7}{15}$

Brain-teaser $\frac{1}{6}$

Brain-buster $\frac{16}{77}$

Page 37

1   **a.** 10 **b.** 6 **c.** 18 **d.** 10 **e.** 25 **f.** 26

2   **a.** $3\frac{1}{2}$ **b.** $12\frac{1}{2}$ **c.** $13\frac{1}{3}$ **d.** 6 **e.** $7\frac{1}{5}$ **f.** $16\frac{2}{3}$

3   **a.** $\frac{1}{6}$ **b.** $\frac{6}{20}$ or $\frac{3}{10}$ **c.** $\frac{24}{72}$ or $\frac{1}{3}$ **d.** $\frac{20}{30}$ or $\frac{2}{3}$ **e.** $\frac{10}{24}$ or $\frac{5}{12}$

    f. $\frac{40}{35}$ or $1\frac{1}{7}$

Brain-teaser $5\frac{1}{4}$ minutes (or 5 minutes 15 seconds)

Brain-buster $\frac{1}{3600}$

Page 39

1   **a.** right **b.** right **c.** wrong **d.** right **e.** wrong **f.** right

2   **a.** $\frac{1}{4}$ **b.** $\frac{1}{12}$ **c.** $\frac{1}{15}$ **d.** $\frac{1}{6}$ **e.** $\frac{3}{16}$ **f.** $\frac{1}{30}$

Brain-teaser $\frac{1}{14}$ of the whole cake

Brain-buster $\frac{1}{80}$ of the sheet; 3 stickers per child.

Page 41

1   **a.** 0.4 **b.** 0.6 **c.** 0.375

2

Fraction	$\frac{1}{8}$	$\frac{2}{8}$	$\frac{3}{8}$	$\frac{4}{8}$	$\frac{5}{8}$	$\frac{6}{8}$	$\frac{7}{8}$	$\frac{8}{8}$
Decimal	0.125	0.25	0.375	0.5	0.625	0.75	0.875	1 or 1.0

3   $\frac{3}{4} = 0.75$, $\frac{5}{8} = 0.625$, $\frac{4}{5} = 0.8$, $\frac{1}{3} = 0.333$

4   $0.166 = \frac{1}{6}$, $0.4 = \frac{2}{5}$, $0.7 = \frac{7}{10}$, $0.125 = \frac{1}{8}$

Brain-teaser $\frac{5}{6}$ (=0.833)

Brain-buster He is wrong. $\frac{1}{12} = 0.083$ and $\frac{1}{10} = 0.1$

Page 43

1   **a.** 0.375: 5 thousandths, 7 hundredths, 3 tenths
    b. 0.903: 3 thousandths, 0 hundredths, 9 tenths

2

Fraction	Decimal	3dps	2dps	1 dps
$\frac{2}{7}$	0.285714	0.286	0.29	0.3
$\frac{3}{13}$	0.230769	0.231	0.23	0.2
$\frac{4}{11}$	0.363636	0.364	0.36	0.4
$\frac{2}{3}$	0.666666	0.667	0.67	0.7
$\frac{8}{9}$	0.888888	0.889	0.89	0.9

Brain-teaser Jared is wrong. It would be rounded down to zero point zero.
Brain-teaser It is a recurring number because 3 ÷ 11 is 0.272727. Rounded to 3dp it is 0.273.

Page 45

1   **a.** 0.6 **b.** 6.6 **c.** 0.92 **d.** 2.04

2   **a.** 4.83 **b.** 6.75 **c.** 6.25 **d.** 109.89

Brain-teaser £9.20
Brain-buster £15.20

Page 46

1   **a.** 0.13 **b.** 0.27 **c.** 0.24

2   **a.** 0.04 **b.** 0.22 **c.** 0.15 **d.** 5.16

Brain-teaser £3.48

Page 47

1

Percentage	Decimal	Fraction
33.3%	0.333	$\frac{1}{3}$
12.5%	0.125	$\frac{1}{8}$
40%	0.4	$\frac{2}{5}$
85%	0.85	$\frac{17}{20}$
87.5%	0.875	$\frac{7}{8}$

Brain-teaser 40%

RATIO AND PROPORTION

Page 49

1   **a.** 4 in 9 or $\frac{4}{9}$ **b.** 1 in 2 or $\frac{1}{2}$ **c.** 1 in 5 or $\frac{1}{5}$

2   **a.** 1:2 **b.** 1:2 **c.** 3:4

Brain-teaser a. 1 in 5 can speak two languages
b. dual to single = 1:4
Brain-buster a. 20 blueberries
b. The proportion of blueberries will be 4 in 7

Page 51

1   **a.** 25% **b.** 70% **c.** 40% **d.** 37.5%

2   **a.** 1 in 4 **b.** 2 in 5 **c.** 13 in 50 **d.** 7 in 8

3   **a.** 50 **b.** 0.5 **c.** 62.4 **d.** 285 **e.** 14.4 **f.** 54

4   See glossary on pages 94 and 95

Brain-teaser 55 cars
Brain-buster 7,560,000 dogs

Page 53

1   **a.** 8cm **b.** 20cm **c.** 40cm

2

Scale	Side length	Area
5:1	5cm	25cm²
10:1	10cm	100cm²
25:1	25cm	625cm²

3   **a.** 50cm **b.** 20cm **c.** 5cm

Brain-teaser 5.5m or 550cm
Brain-buster 7.5:1

ALGEBRA

Page 55

1

Length	Width	P	A
5cm	2cm	14cm	10cm²
5m	4m	18m	20m²
7km	1.5km	17km	10.5km²
3.2m	2.3m	11m	7.36m²

2

h	11	14	20	35	308
f	1	2	4	9	100

Brain-teaser $334
Brain-buster

Fahrenheit	32°	104°	212°
Celsius	0°	40°	100°

Page 57

1 **a.** 8 **b.** 18 **c.** 25 **d.** –2 **e.** 6 **f.** 7 **g.** 4 **h.** 33

2 **a.** 62 **b.** 6 **c.** 10 **d.** –3

Brain-teaser $n = £42.50 - (25 \times £1.50)$
$n = £5$
Brain-buster $n = (190.40 \div 2) \div 5.60$
$n = 17$ children

Page 59

1 **a.**

x	0	1	2	3	4	5	–1	–2	–3
y	2	3	4	5	6	7	1	0	–1

b.

s	0	2	5	6	7	8	9	10	–1
t	8	6	3	2	1	0	–1	–2	9

c.

q	0	1	1.5	2	5	10	100	–1	–10
p	–3	–1	0	1	7	17	197	–5	–23

Brain-teaser a. 60 **b.** 85
Brain-buster $x = 6$, $y = 2$

MEASUREMENT

Page 61

1 **a.** 300 minutes **b.** 7200 seconds

   c. $8\frac{1}{2}$ minutes or 8.5 minutes **d.** 86,400 seconds

2 **a.** 23,000mm **b.** 2400m **c.** 100,000cm **d.** 0.685m

3 **a.** 0.75kg **b.** 32,500g **c.** 0.001kg **d.** 350g

4 **a.** 2500ml **b.** 0.75l **c.** 63.425l **d.** 250ml

Brain-teaser 242 metres 63 centimetres and 7 millimetres
Brain-buster 31,622,400 seconds

Page 63

Brain-teaser 18.75 seconds   0.79kg or 790g   233g
Brain-buster Height = 1m 49.86cm Weight = 39.498kg
29,220 days   701,280 hours   42,076,800 minutes

Page 65

1 **a.** P = 13cm A = 9cm² **b.** P = 6cm A = 2.25cm²

2 **a.** P = 50m A = 87.5m² **b.** P = 24m A = 13.75m²

Brain-teaser 15m²
Brain-buster 180 tiles

Page 67

1 **a.** 10cm² **b.** 17.5cm² **c.** 22.5cm²

2 **a.** square **b.** triangle **c.** triangle

Brain-teaser £511.98
Brain-buster 7.875m²

Page 69

1 **a.** and **b.** Check that children's drawings are accurate.

2 **a.** 216cm³ **b.** 36m³ **c.** 1000m³ **d.** 90cm³
   e. 1728mm³ **f.** 9000mm³

3 1,000,000,000 (one billion)

Brain-teaser 0.125m³, 125,000cm³
Brain-buster 42m³

GEOMETRY

Page 71

1 **a.** right angle **b.** acute angle **c.** obtuse angle

2 **a.** 90° **b.** 143° **c.** 25°

Brain-teaser All acute angles should be 55°;
all obtuse angles 125°
Brain-buster Look for understanding that parallel lines have
similar angles when intersected and that angles on a straight
line add up to 180. The formula might be along the lines of
$2a + 2b = 360°$

Page 73

1 A regular polygon has all sides and angles equal.

2 **a.** equilateral triangle – regular
   b. rhombus (quadrilateral) – irregular
   c. pentagon – irregular **d.** square – regular
   e. hexagon – regular **f.** heptagon – irregular

Brain-teaser The distance from the centre to each corner is
identical, and the four angles at the centre are all 90°.
Brain-buster She is right. The angle at the centre must be 60°
for each triangle, and the side lengths from the centre must be
identical, therefore the other angles must also be 60°, and the
other side an identical length.

Page 75

1 Check that all sides and angles are the same.

2 Check that angle is 120° and all sides are 3cm.

3 Construct an isosceles triangle with single angle =
   360 ÷ 8 = 45°; repeat this 8 times, with the 45° angles
   forming a complete turn in the centre of the octagon.

Brain-teaser 1440°
Brain-buster $a = (n \times 180 - 360) \div n$

Page 77

1 Check that all sides are connected by one tab.

2 Check that net would fold and glue correctly.

Brain-teaser Check that instructions show understanding of faces
joining and dimensions of sides being correct.
Brain-buster a. 5cm × 5cm × 20cm **b.** 150cm² wasted
c. 500cm³

Page 79

1 **a.** radius: the distance from the centre of a circle to the
   circumference
   b. diameter: the distance across the widest part of a circle,
   twice the radius
   c. circumference: the distance around the edge of a circle.

2 7m

3 0.75km or 750m

Brain-teaser No. The circumference of a circle is in fact 3.14d, in
this case = 12.56cm
Brain-buster Yes. The area of a circle is in fact 3.14r², which in
this case = 12.56cm²

1   **a.** A (3, 2) B (−5, 2) C (−5, −6) D (3, −6)   **b.** Square
      c. (−1, −2)

2   **a.** P (3, 5) Q (−1, 5) R (−4, −1) S (0, −1)   **b.** Parallelogram

Brain-teaser A kite
Brain-buster In no particular order, (−3, 6), 2nd quadrant;
(−3, −4), 3rd quadrant; (7, −4), 4th quadrant.

Page 83

1   **a.** P¹(−9, 0) Q¹(−4, 0) R¹(−9, −5) S¹(−4, −5)
      b. W¹(−3, 7) X¹(−9, 7) Y¹(−9, 4) Z¹(−3, 4)
      c. W¹(3, −7) X¹(9, −7) Y¹(9, −4) Z¹(3, −4)

2   A¹(6, −2) B¹(0, −5) C¹(−1, 3)

3   D¹(−2, −4) E¹(1, −7) F¹(−3, −6)

Brain-teaser The reflected square sits on top of the original
square, with the coordinates for P and S swapped, and Q and R
swapped.
Brain-buster Sort of(!) The square will end up in the same place
by reflection or translation, but the vertices will have changed
positions.

STATISTICS

Page 85

1

Cats	Guinea pigs	Dogs	Horses	Hamsters
24	12	6	3	3

2   Use a protractor to check the angles on the pie chart.
      (1p = 1°)

Mum	Dad	Paul	Lizzie	Mary
180°	5°	45°	120°	10°

Brain-teaser Around 40°

Brain-buster Accept answers + or − 0.3 billion.

Asia	Africa	Europe	Oceania	North America	South America
4.2 billion	1 billion	0.7 billion	0.04 billion	0.6 billion	0.5 billion

Page 87

1   **a.** The walkers are not moving.   **b.** 5km   **c.** 7.5km/h
      d.

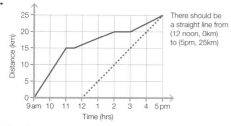

There should be
a straight line from
(12 noon, 0km)
to (5pm, 25km)

      e. 5km/h

Brain-teaser 212°F
Brain-buster x-axis: 32°F, y-axis: −18°C (answers may not be
exact due to the scale of the graph.)

Page 89

1   8

2   **a.** 145 **b.** 24.17

Brain-teaser 56
Brain-buster **a.** average = 274.5 words per page **b.** 103,212

Glossary

12-hour clock Uses 12 hours, with am before 12 noon, and pm after.

24-hour clock Uses 24 hours for the time; does not need am or pm, such as 17:30 = 5.30pm.

2D Two-dimensional, a term used for a shapes with no depth, usually drawn on paper.

3D Three-dimensional, a term used for solid shapes with length, depth and height.

A

Acute angle An angle between 0° and 90°.

Adjacent Near to, or next to, something. Usually used for talking about angles, sides or faces as the properties of a shape.

Algebra The use of symbols to represent numbers.

Analogue clock Shows the time with hands on a dial.

Angle The measure of the gap between lines or of rotation, measured in degrees.

Anti-clockwise Rotating in the opposite direction to the hands of a clock.

Approximate A number found by rounding or estimating.

Area The amount of surface covered by a shape.

Axis (plural axes) The horizontal and vertical lines on a graph.

B

Base 10 The structure of our number system, also called 100s, 10s, 1s and Powers of 10.

C

Circumference The edge of a circle, which is always the same distance from the centre.

Clockwise Rotating in the same direction as the hands of a clock.

Coordinates Numbers that give the position of a point on a graph, (x, y).

Cube number A number multiplied by itself twice, such as $2 \times 2 \times 2 = 2^3 = 8$.

D

Decimal places The position of numbers to the right of the decimal point. Tenths, hundredths, and so on.

Decimal point The dot used to separate the fractional part of a number from the whole.

Denominator The number on the bottom of a fraction.

Diameter The maximum distance across a circle. The diameter is two times the radius.

Difference The amount between two numbers.

Digits Our number system uses ten digits, 0–9, to represent all our numbers.

Digital clock Shows time using digits rather than by having hands on a dial, often uses 24-hour time.

E

Edge The line where two faces of a 3D shape meet.

Equation A sentence of numbers, variables and operations that balances about the = sign.

Equivalent fractions Two or more fractions where the same amount is represented differently, such as $\frac{1}{2}$ and $\frac{2}{4}$.

Estimate To use information to get an approximate answer.

Even numbers Whole numbers that can be divided by 2. They end in 0, 2, 4, 6 or 8.

F

Face The flat or curved areas of 3D shapes.

Factor A number that will divide exactly into a particular number. 4 is a factor of 12.

Formula An equation used for calculating particular quantities, such as the area of a circle.

I

Imperial units Traditional units for measuring length, capacity, mass, such as pints and ounces.

Improper fraction (or vulgar fraction) A fraction with a larger numerator than denominator.

Irregular polygon A 2D shape which does not have identical sides and angles.

Isometric A drawing: a technique for drawing 3D shapes on flat surfaces.

L

Line graph A graph used to show changes over time, such as height, temperature or speed.

M

Mean The average of a set of data. The total divided by the number of items.

Mental methods Approaches for accurately solving calculations without writing them down.

Million The number 1,000,000; one thousand times one thousand.

Mixed number The combination of a whole number and a fraction, such as $3\frac{2}{5}$.

Multiple A number made by multiplying two numbers together. 6 is a multiple of 2, and also a multiple of 3.

N

Negative number A number less than zero.

Numerator The top number of a fraction. The numerator is divided by the denominator.

O

Obtuse angle An angle between 90° and 180°.

Odd numbers Whole numbers that cannot be divided exactly by 2. They end in 1, 3, 5, 7 or 9.

P

Percentage A number expressed as a fraction out of 100, such as 58%.

Perimeter The distance around the edge of a closed shape.

Pie chart Data represented as proportions of 360°, shown as fractions of a circle.

Polygon Any straight-sided 2D shape.

Positive number A number greater than zero.

Powers of ten The structure of our number system, also called Base 10 or 100s, 10s, 1s.

Prime factor A factor that is also a prime number. 3 is a prime factor of 12.

Prime number A whole number that can only be divided exactly by itself and 1.

Proportion The fraction of an amount, such as eight out of nine people wore red.

Q

Quadrants The four sections of a coordinate grid, positive and negative.

R

Radius The distance from the centre of a circle to the circumference.

Range The difference between the smallest and largest numbers in a data set.

Ratio The comparison of quantities, such as there is one black bead for every three white.

Recurring decimal A decimal that repeats the same number or numbers forever.

Reflection Changing the coordinates of a point or shape in a mirror line.

Reflex angle An angle measuring between 180° and 360°.

Regular polygon A 2D shape with all sides and angles identical.

Roman numerals The system of letters used by the Romans to represent numbers.

Rounding To simplify a number to the nearest power of 10.

S

Square number A number multiplied by itself, such as $3 \times 3 = 9$.

Symbol A sign used for an operation or relationship in mathematics, such as +, −, ×, ÷ or =, <, >.

Symmetrical A symmetrical shape is one that is identical either side of a mirror line.

T

Translation To move the coordinates of a point or shape, by the same amounts, on a graph.

V

Vertex (plural vertices) The corner of a 3D shape where edges meet.

Multiplication table

x	1	2	3	4	5	6	7	8	9	10	11	12
1	1	2	3	4	5	6	7	8	9	10	11	12
2	2	4	6	8	10	12	14	16	18	20	22	24
3	3	6	9	12	15	18	21	24	27	30	33	36
4	4	8	12	16	20	24	28	32	36	40	44	48
5	5	10	15	20	25	30	35	40	45	50	55	60
6	6	12	18	24	30	36	42	48	54	60	66	72
7	7	14	21	28	35	42	49	56	63	70	77	84
8	8	16	24	32	40	48	56	64	72	80	88	96
9	9	18	27	36	45	54	63	72	81	90	99	108
10	10	20	30	40	50	60	70	80	90	100	110	120
11	11	22	33	44	55	66	77	88	99	110	121	132
12	12	24	36	48	60	72	84	96	108	120	132	144